Movement
and
Meaning

Movement

and

Meaning

Eleanor Metheny

McGraw-Hill Book Company   *New York, St. Louis,*
San Francisco, Toronto, London, Sydney

Movement
and
Meaning

The squirming facts exceed the
squamous mind,
If one may say so. And yet
relation appears. . . .

Wallace Stevens

PREFACE

. . . the edgings and inchings of final form

In our time, the pursuit of knowledge in all fields of inquiry has been transformed into a search for the sources of meaning in human life. In *Movement and Meaning*, this search is focused on the act of moving, with particular reference to the forms of movement called dance, sport, and exercise.

The concept of *forms*, which was proposed by Ernst Cassirer some fifty years ago, is now the central theme of inquiries in all fields of knowledge. This was evidenced as early as 1951, when Lancelot Law Whyte brought together the papers of a dozen fields under the title *Aspects of Form*. In the Preface to this collection, Herbert Read identified the concept of forms as "the unitary principle which is emerging as the explanation of all phenomena within the range of human perception and understanding."

Movement and Meaning begins with an exposition of that principle as it relates to the search for meaning in all nonverbal forms of behavior. Then this principle is developed within an analysis of the sources of meaning in the forms called dance, sport, exercise, and education.

In general, then, this book is offered as a contribution to the growing body of literature that deals with nonverbal forms of human understanding. More specifically, it is directed to those readers who have a primary interest in movement forms.

Movement and Meaning has been a long time in the writing. Its central theme was suggested by the works of Ernst Cassirer and Susanne K. Langer. This theme was explored in the contemporary literature of philosophy, psychology, neurophysiology, and education. It was clarified in discussions with countless colleagues and students. Various aspects of it were explicated in a long series of papers, partially collected in 1965 under the title *Connotations of Movement in Sport and Dance.* Some of these papers, and all the ideas in them, were developed in an ongoing collaboration with Lois Elizabeth Ellfeldt of the University of Southern California. My intellectual debts to her are beyond verbal description; here let me say only that our long collaboration on the ideas set forth in *Movement and Meaning* has been the most rewarding interaction of my professional life.

My debts to other colleagues are also gratefully acknowledged. Here, special mention is made of those who met with us in the mountains of Colorado in 1958 and those who participated in the Colloquy on Movement and Meaning held at Idyllwild Arts Foundation in 1959. But I am also indebted to countless others who engaged in the dialogue of dozens of workshops and other conferences.

Special mention must also be made of the younger colleagues who participated in the seminars on movement theory I have offered at the University of Southern California since 1960. Vigorously and courageously, these students challenged my thinking, even as they offered me their own insights into the meanings they found in dance, sport, and exercise. For this, I shall be forever in their debt.

The long process of developing *Movement and Meaning* was supported in part by a grant from the Amy Morris Homans Fund of Wellesley College, in 1962. It was also supported by two sabbatical leaves granted by my own university.

For the present organization of the book, I am indebted to the University of Illinois for an opportunity to present a series of lectures in 1965. In these lectures, I reorganized the diffuse thinking of many years around my initial interest in Ernst Cassirer's concept of forms. The transcripts of these lectures provided the outline for *Movement and Meaning*.

In its present form, the book might be used as a text or reference in courses concerned with the theoretical foundations of physical education. I hope that it will serve this purpose and that its contents will be meaningful to both undergraduate and graduate students. It might also be used as a reference in courses in philosophy, education, art, or any other discipline that has a presumptive interest in nonverbal forms of meaning. But if it serves only these purposes, I shall have failed of my larger intent.

The important meanings of dance, sport, and exercise are not found in the writings of philosophers. Neither are they limited to the purview of education. Rather, they are found in the lives of the millions of people who find their own involvement in dance, sport, or exercise meaningful.

As I pursued my theoretical search for the sources of meaning in dance, sport, and exercise, I found that my personal involvement in these movement forms became increasingly meaningful to me. And so I hope that *Movement and Meaning* will find many readers who are involved in dance, sport, and exercise in their own way and for their own personal reasons—as performers, as spectators, and as commentators and critics.

To them, I dedicate this book, in the hope that they, too, may come to find more meaning in their own involvement in movement forms.

Eleanor Metheny

CONTENTS

Movement
and
Meaning

CHAPTER 1

FORMS

A definition with an illustration, not
Too exactly labelled.

Men find meaning in their own lives by recognizing the patterns of reality in many forms. This book is concerned with the meanings we may find in the patterns of four very complex forms, commonly called dance, sport, exercise, and education. But it starts with the simpler question: How do men find meaning in the form called a *chalk stick*?

A stick of chalk may be called a form because it is much more than a random assemblage of chalk particles. It is an organization of particles, arranged in such a way that they stick together as a coherent and functional whole. As we look at or handle this stick, we can recognize it for what it is, which is to say that we can reconstruct some representation of it within our own awareness of the forms of reality.

What kind of materials did we use to formulate this cognitive image of the chalk stick? This question has not yet been answered in the categorical terms of science, but to give these materials a name, so that we can talk about them, let us call them *perceptual elements*. And if we must verify the existence of such elements, let us call upon our own experiences in recognizing many forms within the universe of our existence in this way.

We may define a *perceptual form*, then, as a coherent arrangement or organization of perceptual elements which is cognized as a structural and functional whole and identified as an entity in its own right. Such a perceptual form has a 1 to 1 relationship with the material form which was perceived. It is the perceptual form which corresponds to our recognition of that particular stick of chalk. But your perceptual form is not necessarily the same as mine. Each of us has observed the chalk stick from his own particular point of view and within the context of his own interest at the moment. Therefore a perceptual form always has certain individual characteristics which have personal, but not necessarily general, validity.

Having cognized the chalk stick as a perceptual form, we may find it of sufficient interest to warrant closer examination, or we may pay no further attention to it. If we observe it more closely, we may note that the chalk stick has recognizable boundaries which set it apart from the other aspects of reality that surround it. These boundaries serve to establish our awareness of its shape or external configuration; and as we interest ourselves in this configuration, we find that we can deal with a conception of this shape, as such, apart from the stick of chalk in which we discovered it.

We may test this observation by looking for this same *configuration* in other forms not made of chalk, noting that it may be identified in the forms called pencil, cigarette, and finger, but not in the form called notebook. Apparently, then, we can entertain a conception of configuration, as such, without reference to the materials which may be used to shape it. This conception about how materials are organized, which was *abstracted from* our observations of many organizations of materials, may be called a *conceptual form*.

The number and variety of conceptual forms which may be abstracted from our recognition of a material form are limited only by our interest and powers of observation. By focusing our attention on different aspects of the chalk stick, we may abstract a conception of hardness, or a conception of whiteness, or a conception of flakiness—each representing a pattern of organization which we might recognize in other material forms.

We may also be interested in the functional properties of this cylindrical, hard, white, flaky chalk form. Then we may abstract a conception of the function of mark making, and we may note how each of the structural components is related to this function. A cylinder of this size and weight may be held in the fingers, comfortably, and without need for great effort. The stick is hard enough to hold together as we pick it up, and the chalk particles cohere to such an extent that they do not rub off on our fingers, but the stick is also soft enough to yield to pressure against a hard surface, and particles of chalk are separated from the form by such pressure, remaining on the blackboard to trace distinctive white configurations which we recognize as letters, words, and diagrams.

We now have a very complex set of conceptions about the chalk stick. From a structural point of view, we have noted the materials (chalk particles) and how they are organized in relation to each other (compressed, stuck together, stick form). From a functional point of view, we have noted the operational characteristics of this structure (particles separate from stick under pressure but not when stick is lightly held), and we have noted how the stick functions as an organized whole (as a mark maker) and how this function is related to the structural-functional relationships within the stick. All these conceptions are brought together in the conceptual form denoted by the term *chalk stick*.

This conceptual form is a conception of all the structural-functional relationships we have recognized within the form and between the form and its surroundings. For convenience, we shall use only the first letters of *S*tructure, *F*unction, and *R*elationship and call this a conception of the SFRs we have identified in the form.

Our conception of this set of SFRs may be vague. We might, for example, recognize the chalk form as being "something like a finger." However, if we examine it more closely, we may recognize the organizational patterns of roundness, smoothness, length, whiteness, and chalkiness. Then we might refer to our conception as an *idea* about how the form is organized, or an idea about a set of SFRs. But if we study it very carefully, trying to identify the SFRs which distinguish chalk-stick mark makers from all other kinds of mark makers, we might call our recognition of these relationships a well-developed *concept* about the nature of chalk sticks.

These distinctions between conception, idea, and concept are relative rather than categorical. A conception might be described as a vague idea about some pattern of organization; a fairly well-defined idea might be described as a general concept. We shall not quibble here about precise distinctions among these terms. Rather, we shall use them to suggest degrees of clarity in our understanding of the SFRs we recognize within the grand design of reality.

Any conception, however vague, may be *meaningful* to us; similarly, any concept, however clearly recognized, may be virtually *meaningless*. This distinction does not rest on clarity of recognition; it rests on our *interest* in whatever we have recognized.

At times we may recognize an idea, and we may have some understanding of it, but if it does not arouse our interest at that moment, we pay little attention to it. Another idea, which we may or may not fully understand, may immediately engage our interest. Then, we will involve ourselves in that idea by focusing our attention on it. In this sense we may say that we are *affected* by the idea, because our recognition of it has served to bring about a reorganization of the components of our own being.

This *affective* feeling of being interested may be subtle and difficult to describe, or we may be fully aware of it. It may be experienced as nothing more than a momentary fluctuation of our interest in ourselves and our relationships within the world of our existence, or it may be experienced as a fully organized emotional state, accompanied by all the observable physiological changes which are associated with excitement, feeling, and emotion. But subtle or explicit, it is experienced as some degree of personal involvement with the conception. Or we may say that this sense of involvement with the conception marks the difference between knowing about a pattern of organization and experiencing that recognition as a conception that affects our own being in some significant way.

No form is innately meaningful, in and of itself; neither is any conception of its organizational patterns innately meaningful. Rather, this conception becomes meaningful to us as we seize upon it, take it into ourselves, and become involved with it. This feeling of involvement is a symptom of what the idea *means* to us, or how we find it meaningful or significant.

We may explore this conception of significance or meaning by asking how we construct forms of our own devising. To illustrate this process, we might use some aluminum foil, which was itself constructed by this form-making process.

If a person attempts to create a form by manipulating a sheet of aluminum foil, he might just fumble around with it, pushing it here, crumbling it there, squeezing it with his fingers in the hope that something of interest might emerge from the process. Possibly it would, but more likely such random manipulation would produce only a random crumpling of the material. To create a significant form, he must begin with some conception of a significant set of SFRs.

This initial thought may be either a conception of structural configuration or a conception of function. Perhaps a person is intrigued by a vague conception of a bit of space partially surrounded by some solid material. Or perhaps he has a stack of small objects which he wants to keep together, and he is considering how this might be accomplished. As he ponders the SFRs of a form which might serve this purpose, he may begin to experiment with the foil, pushing it this way and that, squeezing it in here, smoothing it there, using his own energies to change its configuration and impose new SFRs upon it.

Since his conception of these SFRs is still rather vague, the first version of his man-made form may be rather vaguely structured. Perhaps it is little more than a lump of foil with a depression in one side. But as he puts it down with the depressed side uppermost and puts several short pieces of chalk stick in the hollow, he can observe that the structure imposed on the foil does, in fact, serve the function of containing several small objects and holding them together.

Now that this person has an idea about what he is trying to make, he can organize his materials more effectively. Taking a fresh sheet of foil, he can organize it into a functional container, perhaps shaping it around his fist to maintain a hollow in the form. This second version of the form probably works better than the first, because he now has a clearer idea of both structure and function.

If he shows you his man-made form, you may or may not recognize his idea. You may recognize it as a structure without conceiving of its possible functions. Or you may recognize it only as an uninteresting blob of aluminum foil and pay no attention to it. You may also recognize certain subpatterns of organization in the form, noting that it is round rather than square, rough rather than smooth, shiny rather than dull, and hollow rather than solid. Or perhaps you will turn it upside down and recognize it as a form which might function as a head cover or skullcap. Or your interest may lead you to ask: What is it?

Obviously, it is a form made of aluminum foil. Assuming that you can recognize foil when you see it, there is no need for you to ask: What is it? What you really want to know is: What idea does this form represent? Now he can reply: "It represents my idea of a 'container' or a form which can perform the function of containing."

But knowingly or unknowingly, this person has also incorporated into the form many other subsidiary patterns which you may recognize as roundness, roughness, and shiny color. These patterns are not necessarily relevant to his idea of a form that can perform the function of containing. As he tries to explain this to you and to himself, he begins to sort out the relevant SFRs which are essential to his emerging concept of a container, and he understands his own idea more clearly.

Having arrived at a reasonably well-organized concept of "a form that can perform the function of containing other forms," he can expand and further clarify that concept by introducing new elements into its organizational pattern. He can conceive of a container which might be particularly well adapted to the function of transporting water from place to place, another which would keep coffee hot while also facilitating the process of pouring, and another which might be used to store jewels or money. With each new application of the basic concept, his understanding of these SFRs is expanded and clarified, and the concept becomes simultaneously more complex and better understood. It also becomes more meaningful to him, because he discovers that it has many implications for his life.

Any such man-made form may also serve another very important purpose. The idea of a set of SFRs which might represent some conception of containing was originally developed within the private realms of a person's thoughts. In making a form which exhibits those SFRs, he has, in effect, externalized his idea and made it available to you. He did this by imposing a set of SFRs on tangible material in such a way that the form he created served to represent his idea. Or we may say that the tangible form serves to *denote* that idea.

If we choose to give this form a name, perhaps calling it *bowl*, this word name may also be said to denote the idea which the bowl represents. Using this word name, we may talk about the specific bowl made of aluminum foil, calling it *the* bowl, or we may refer to the idea or concept of bowls in general by speaking of *a* bowl.

We may note that the word *bowl* is itself a man-made form. We made it by shaping a little puff of air into a recognizable sound. But the relationship between this *word form* and the idea it denotes is not the same as the relationship between the idea and the tangible bowl. The denotational relationship between word and idea is purely conventional. Any other word sound, such as *pot, basket,* or *thingamajig,* could have served our purpose of denoting the bowl idea if we had agreed to use it in this way. In contrast, the relationship between the actual bowl and the idea it denotes is implicit in the construction of the bowl, because the bowl was constructed by combining the idea and the material.

We may recognize this important distinction by calling the word which serves to denote the idea of a bowl a *verbal form*, while describing the bowl itself as a *presentational form*, or a form which presents or exhibits a specific set of SFRs directly in its own construction.

Any form, either verbal or presentational, may serve to denote a conception, an idea, or a concept. It may also serve to suggest other conceptions, ideas, or concepts, which are said to be *connoted* rather than *denoted* by the form. Such connoted ideas or connotations may be evoked by recognition of some similarity between the SFRs of the form and certain other form-defining sets of SFRs. Thus, recognition of the bowl might suggest a skullcap. Or these connoted ideas might be evoked by recognition of some subpattern in the form which exhibits or suggests a set of SFRs observed in other forms. Thus, the silver color of the bowl might suggest silver or coins or a container for storing silver coins. Recognition of the functional utility of the bowl as a container of water might serve to suggest the idea of needing water or being thirsty. The appearance or configuration of the bowl might suggest ideas about forms of similar configuration. Or perhaps the specific bowl was first used in a situation which is recalled by our immediate recognition of the bowl. These connotational conceptions, ideas, and concepts cannot be predicted for any given form. In this sense, each man's connotations are his own and so are the meanings he finds in them.

Verbal forms, such as the word *bowl*, may also connote as well as denote conceptions, ideas, and concepts. Here we have used the word sound *bowl* to denote the idea of a round, rather shallow container. By virtue of this sound pattern, it may also suggest the idea of *ball* or perhaps the idea of *roll*. Or it may suggest the act of bowling or perhaps the configuration of the sky as "the blue bowl of the heavens." Verbal forms also acquire connotational powers by association with situations and circumstances in which they have been used, so that a seemingly innocuous word may evoke recollection of an emotionally charged experience in which the word, or the idea it represents, played an important role.

Summarizing all these observations about our own experiences in dealing with forms, we have noted that any form— material, perceptual, or conceptual, natural or man made, presentational or verbal—may be considered from three different points of view. We may ask: What materials are used in its construction? How are those materials organized? We may also ask: What conception-idea-concept is *denoted* by this form? Or: What name is commonly assigned to this organization of materials? Or we may ask: What other conceptions-ideas-concepts are *connoted* by this form? Or: What connotations does it have for me?

Each pair of questions will elicit a different set of answers, and each set of answers is valid within the given mode of interpretation. Each mode of interpretation can also evoke some degree of interest, feeling, and emotion, as symptoms of our involvement in the ideas represented by the form. Thus, each mode of interpretation provides one part of the comprehensive answer to the question: In what ways do I find my recognition of this form meaningful? Or: What does this form *mean* to me?

Two or more men may reach agreement on their answers to questions about what a form *is* and what idea it *denotes*. They may agree about the materials and how they are organized, and they may agree about the SFRs denoted by the name they assign to the form. But we cannot expect them to agree about the connotations they may find in a form, because each man must find his own connotations within the context of his own interests, feelings, and emotions. He must also find his own meanings in the form; the form will mean to him whatever it does mean to him, and no other person can either agree or disagree with those meanings.

Any form which serves to evoke a meaningful conception-idea-concept may be called a *symbol*. As a symbol, it has the properties of being, denotation, and connotation, which is to say that the meanings it evokes are susceptible to analysis within each of the three modes of interpretation. At times we may be interested in the material elements of the form and the SFRs which determine their organization. At other times we may be interested in the idea denoted by the fully organized form. And at other times the form may be meaningful because it serves to connote other conceptions-ideas-concepts which are more interesting to us than the denoted idea.

Throughout most of this chapter we have concentrated our attention on two simple symbolic forms, a chalk stick and a crude bowl. Now let us test our understanding of those ideas by relating them to a more complex form which belongs within the realm of sport. Recognition of this form may be conveyed in the statement: A man is throwing a javelin. Or we may identify the form by the term *javelin throw*.

Within the first mode of interpretation, we are able to recognize the materials which enter into the form and the way in which those materials are organized. The materials may be described as a long strip of ground with certain marks on it, a man, and a stick of wood or plastic with a metal point. One set of relationships among these materials is described in a set of rules. The dynamic relationships between the man, the marked ground, and the stick may be described as an organization of movements and forces. As the stick moves through space, the relationships between the stick and the ground may be described as another organization of forces and movements. Taken together, this complex set of SFRs serves to unite man, stick, ground, and space within a recognizable dynamic entity which denotes the idea of a *javelin throw*.

But what other ideas are suggested by our recognition of this dynamic set of SFRs or by our recognition of the various subpatterns of organization within the fully organized form? What connotations do these subpatterns have for us? Perhaps the stick suggests the idea of a spear. Perhaps the throwing pattern suggests the uses which men make of spears in warfare or in hunting. Or we may be interested in the relationship between concepts of distance and direction and the movement-force patterns exhibited by the thrower. What connotations arise from our recognition of the starting line and our awareness of a set of rules governing both the properties of the stick and the man's behavior? What is suggested by the observation that two men who throw javelins from the same starting line under the same rules are interested in comparing the distance covered by their throws? In what way are we interested in our own recognition of the dynamic patterns within this symbolic form of behavior? How do we interpret their relevance to our own concerns? How are we affected by the conceptions-ideas-concepts evoked by our recognition of the form called a *javelin throw*? In short, what does the form mean to us as a symbol or symbolic form of human behavior? What does it mean to the javelin thrower?

The first two modes of interpretation can probably be pursued without argument. Without too much difficulty we can usually agree about materials and patterns of organization and about the idea denoted by this organization of materials. The third mode of interpretation is more speculative, but in the end it is equally unarguable. Each man's connotations are his own, and they are valid for him within the context of his own interests and understanding. A javelin throw is meaningful to you in whatever way it is meaningful to you—but at least we can agree that it *is* meaningful as a symbolic form, because it has the properties of being, denotation, and connotation, and because it has engaged the interest of men for at least three thousand years.

CHAPTER 2

MAN-MADE FORMS

A new text of the world,
A scribble of fret and fear and fate,
From a bravura of the mind . . .
A text of intelligent men
At the center of the unintelligible . . .

We began our exploration of the process of creating new forms by converting a sheet of foil wrap into a container. In this experiment we used a basic idea which was conceived long ago by our earliest human ancestors. Now we may push our thinking about man-made forms a bit farther by asking: Who made the *first* container? How did he devise or develop his original idea? How did he work out this conception in the materials available to him?

As to the identity of this first creator of a man-made bowl form, we can only speculate. To give him a name, let us call him Ug. But we can do more than speculate about the development of this man-made idea and its ultimate materialization as a man-made form. We can trace those stages within the context of our own experiences in devising new ideas and creating new forms.

Ug was a human being. In his own primitive way he was able to formulate his own conceptions about how reality is organized. Those conceptions may have been fuzzy and scarcely comprehended, but they were the hallmark of his right to be called *human*; out of these processes of human thought he fashioned the first man-made forms.

Ug's idea about a bowl-like form grew out of his own experience in perceiving and interacting with natural forms. Like the animals around him, he slaked his thirst by drinking water where he found it—in streams, lakes, springs, water holes, and other hollows in the earth in which rainwater collected. He was familiar, too, with many hollow forms, such as nutshells, clamshells, and cup-shaped leaves. On occasion, he had scooped up water in his cupped hands, and probably he had used shells and leaves to transport water for short distances. He had also rearranged clay with his hands as he dug for clams and grubs, and as he walked in the damp clay, his feet had made depressions which were hardened by the sun.

At this point we might compare Ug with Sir Isaac Newton on that legendary day when he lay in the shade of an apple tree. All the elements needed to formulate the conception of gravity had long been present in Newton's experience. Then, in that historic moment when an apple fell from the tree and struck him on the head, these elements were suddenly brought together within a new context. Or we may say, Newton was suddenly struck by an idea about how the behavior of all material forms is affected by some generalized force which pulls them toward the ground.

But Newton did not jump to his feet crying: "Eureka! I have discovered the idea of gravity." Only much later was he able to trace the beginnings of that idea back to the falling apple. At the moment of initial insight, he did not know what he was thinking about; he knew only that he was vaguely disturbed by something he could not identify.

And so it was with Ug. We do not know what event served to bring his recognition of many familiar elements of experience together within a new context. Perhaps he was far from the water hole and very thirsty. Perhaps a nutshell with a bit of water in it moved when he struck it with his foot. Perhaps he was scooping up water in his dirt-covered hands. In any event, something happened which served to evoke several vague conceptions simultaneously, and these conceptions were bound together in his thinking by a recognition of the common sub-patterns within them. And, like Newton, Ug was disturbed by this experience.

Ug could not talk to himself about this disturbing vague conception because he had not yet invented language. But neither could Newton talk to himself about his feeling of being about to have an idea, because he literally did not know what he was thinking about.

As the poet T. S. Eliot has put it, the development of a new idea begins as "a raid on the inarticulate" conducted within "the messy imprecision of feeling undisciplined squads of emotion." Or as Albert Einstein has observed: "I seldom think in words at all. . . . I work out the idea first . . . and then, much later, I try to explain it in words." In one way or another, we all have experienced this disturbance which characterizes the beginning of some reorganization of our thinking, and so we can call upon our experiences to reconstruct the next stage in Ug's idea-formulating process.

We may picture him sitting under a tree, seemingly oblivious to events occurring around him, because his attention is focused on his own vague thoughts. If we observe him closely, we may note that he is tense and restless. His hands move in quick, jerky patterns which seem to have no purpose. He makes groping and grasping motions; he kicks aimlessly at nothing. He squirms and shakes his head, as if to relieve his feeling of tension. And his eyes seem to dart in all directions, as if he were looking for something without quite knowing what it is or where he might find it.

Perhaps Ug found his idea as he sat under the tree, but more likely he did not. Rather, like Newton, he was probably interrupted by the occurrence of some other event which demanded his attention. Perhaps the sun had set and he recognized that he had to get back to the cave before nightfall. And so we may picture him shaking his head and body and shrugging his shoulders, as if to rid himself of his disturbing thoughts, and directing his attention to the necessity of getting back to the cave.

But that evening, as we picture him sitting by the fire, his disturbance is still apparent. He pays no attention to his cave mates, and perhaps the more perceptive wonder what is the matter with Ug. He picks up a stone and throws it down; he scratches at the floor of the cave with his fingers; and perhaps he picks up a blob of soft clay and tosses it idly back and forth between his hands, squeezing it with his fingers, and hitting it with his fists. And then, suddenly, he is transformed into a purposeful being.

Now his attention is focused on the clay, and his hands and fingers move swiftly. He pats and shapes the clay, now this way, then that way. Then he shakes his head, squashes the clay into a lump, and starts over again. It is now evident that he knows what he is trying to do, but he does not yet know quite how to do it.

As he works, we note that his hands shake with a slight tremor, as if he were trying to find the exact movement he needs; and his eyes move continually over the emerging form, as if he were seeking clues to clarify his conception of the desired pattern. But as he discovers how to move his hands and fingers to shape his idea in the clay, the tremors decrease and his eyes are focused on his work. And gradually, a presentational form emerges which may be described as the materialization of his idea.

We do not know how Ug discovered that his form could be hardened by placing it in the fire. Perhaps he made this discovery by accident, as he put the form aside and went to sleep.

When morning came, he took the hardened form down to the water hole to test its functional properties. Yes, Ug's idea actually held water! But history does not suggest that his companions were impressed by this demonstration. Rather, it is more likely that they felt threatened by Ug's strange behavior and drew away from him and his attempt to reorganize the realities of nature.

But Ug was not dismayed. He had his idea, and he knew that it worked. Therefore he sought to expand his understanding of that idea by making more bowls and pots and containers, each of which served some useful purpose.

In his second attempt to make an idea into a bowl, Ug also sat hunched over his work, and the tension of his intense concentration was evident in the muscles of his back, his legs, his arms, and his contorted face. From time to time he would hesitate, tremble, scan the form with his hands as well as his eyes, and then try a slightly different movement with his fingers. Bit by bit, as his conceptions of the idea, the form, and the movements needed to shape it were simultaneously clarified, the muscles in his legs, back, and neck relaxed, and the movement patterns were centered in his fingers. Now he could look up from his work and interact with his companions while his fingers seemed to move of their own accord. Or we might say, Ug had developed his skill to such an extent that he no longer needed to think about how he was moving his hands.

In time, Ug's companions were persuaded that bowls were useful to man, and some of them undertook to make their own containers. Their first attempts were clumsy; they, too, exhibited tension in their backs and legs as they worked; and from time to time they hesitated, trembled, and then scanned the clay with their hands as well as with their eyes. But from Ug, the teacher, they had learned much about the general pattern of the necessary finger movements, and so they were able to develop their skill more readily. Soon they, too, were able to turn out one clay pot after another almost without thinking.

The more alert, more curious, and more inventive form makers found much to interest them as they worked with these symbolic bowls. Some were interested in the materials, how they were organized, and how they functioned; others were more interested in the ideas denoted by the forms they made; and still others were more interested in the ideas connoted by these patterns of organization. These interests gave meaning to their work and to their conceptions of themselves as men who could reorganize the materials of nature into new and man-made forms. To give these interested workers a name, so that we may talk about them, let us call them Sci, Ven, Pat, and Fil.

Sci's interest in symbolic forms was centered in the first mode of interpretation. As he worked the clay with his hands, he rubbed bits of it between his fingers, feeling its texture and noting how it crumbled into tiny particles as it dried and how it stuck together when it was damp or when it was baked in the fire. He asked the scientist's questions: What? How?

What is clay? What is it made of? What is water? Dust? Heat? How are the particles of water and dust bound together to form a sticky mass? What is roundness? How is it different from straightness? What are the SFRs within a circular rim? What are my hands made of? How are these materials organized to make a functional hand which responds to my attempt to shape the clay?

Ven's attention was focused on the second mode of inter-pretation. He was interested in the functional properties of bowls and the ways in which men might use them. As he worked the clay with his hands, he speculated about the possibility of putting an indentation in the circular rim to facilitate pouring and tried adding a projecting lump of clay to hold on to, and perhaps he bent the sides inward at the top and devised the idea of making a cover that would fit inside the circular rim. Each of these innovations changed the structure of the form in ways which denoted the specific functions assigned to the bowl. Thus, we may say that Ven worked to clarify the relationship between the structural and functional properties of the form and the specific idea denoted by them.

Sci's name suggests his interest in the questions of science; Ven's name suggests his interest in inventing new forms to serve men's needs and interests. But what about Pat?

Pat was also an inventive worker, but he had little interest in the questions of utility. He preferred the third mode of interpretation. As he worked the clay with his hands, he was fascinated by the patterns of organization he recognized within the clay forms. He studied the configuration of his bowls and asked: Is this shape pleasing or displeasing? What feelings does it evoke? What connotations does it have for me?

Pat experimented with changing the proportions of the bowls, seeking pleasing and satisfying patterns and designs. He also noted that consideration of certain patterns could evoke ideas about how other aspects of reality were organized and some sense of how he felt about these things. A wavy line might evoke the idea of waves rippling in the sun as the wind moved the waters of the lake; or the rhythmic pattern of an undulating line might suggest the rhythms of his own life as he experienced day-night, summer-winter, birth-death. As he worked these patterns into his clay forms or traced them on the surfaces of the bowls he was making, sometimes he used them to denote ideas as well as to evoke recognition of related ideas and feelings, but he was not greatly concerned about the denotational properties of his bowls. Rather, as an artist, he sought to enhance and intensify the connotational powers of these symbolic patterns.

Sci and Ven and Pat worked side by side at their symbol-

making tasks, each intent on his own chosen mode of interpretation, and it seems likely that they did not always share each other's interests and preoccupations. Or perhaps they had simply not yet discovered how to communicate their ideas to each other. Eventually Fil found a uniquely human solution to that problem.

As Fil worked the clay with his hands, he often thought about what he was doing, but more often he found himself thinking about other emerging conceptions, ideas, and concepts. As he tried to sort these out and put them in some kind of order, he found he needed some kind of material form to denote them. Grunting and groaning and mumbling to himself while he worked, he found those symbols in his own mouth and throat. He discovered that he could move his face, lips, tongue, larynx, and rib cage in such a way as to shape little puffs of air into recognizable sounds, such as *awk*, *glub*, and *bowl*. Then, by establishing a connection between a sound and an idea, he could use that sound to denote that idea. And in time he discovered that he could also denote the relationships between ideas by arranging his words in various ways. Thus, *man-kill-animal* denoted one set of relationships, and *animal-kill-man* denoted a very different set of SFRs.

Equipped with this man-made system of verbal forms, Fil was able to sort out his emerging conceptions, ideas, and concepts and, in effect, diagram the relationships he recognized within them. Or we may say that his thinking was made more articulate, because he could identify the connections or articulations which seemed to join his ideas together within a more comprehensive pattern.

As Sci, Ven, and Pat learned to relate recognizable word sounds to ideas, they found a convenient way to communicate with each other about those ideas. For example, if Sci wanted Ven to think about the process of running, he no longer had to demonstrate what he meant by creating a presentational form of his idea. He had only to move his lips and tongue to form the word *run*. In this way the men could communicate with each other without interrupting their work, or when their backs were turned toward each other, or when they were separated by space or darkness.

In time, they discovered that they could also make marks which would represent these word sounds, and the possibilities for communication were greatly extended. Now abstracted ideas could be preserved and transmitted through space and time as separate entities which had their own existence apart from the man who thought about them, so that they might be used by many men who never saw each other face to face.

Verbal forms, both oral and written, were used to denote ideas; but as men used them in this way, words also acquired many connotations. Thus, the word sound *cat* might denote the idea of a furry four-legged animal, but to the man who used it in this way, it also connoted his feelings about such animals and some sense of his own relationship to them in many situations. In this sense, the *meaning* each man found in, or attached to, the verbal symbol became a very complex conception of what a cat is and how he feels about cats. Since each man's connotations are his own, the word *cat* did not have precisely the same meaning for any two men; and communication among men was often blocked by their inability to recognize each other's meanings.

Nonetheless, as men equipped themselves with verbal forms, they found their lives expanding in all directions. Sci could communicate his ever-increasing insights into the SFRs of nature to other men who could use those ideas to facilitate their own discovery of new insights. Ven could communicate his ever-increasing ideas about how man might reorganize the SFRs of nature in ways that would serve his own interests, and other men could use those ideas to develop new conceptions of forms which would function in new ways. And Pat and Fil could communicate their ever-increasing understanding of themselves, their feelings, and their thoughts to other men who might expand that understanding.

Generation by generation, the descendants of Ug moved

farther from the cave into the larger community of human culture and human civilization. In the same way that Ug had conceived of the idea of a portable water container and made it work, Sci, Ven, Pat, Fil and their descendants devised new material forms and new forms of human interaction called social institutions, governments, laws, and universities.

This may seem a long way to travel with one crude bowl, but the process of reorganizing the natural materials of the universe into man-made forms is the same for the invention of the United Nations as it was for the clay pot. It begins with the peculiarly human process of "getting an idea"; it proceeds by virtue of man's ability to translate the SFRs he recognizes within that idea into material forms which exhibit those structural-functional relationships. He accomplishes this translation of idea into substantial form by moving with and against the SFRs of the universe.

As Socrates thought about these things many centuries ago, he recognized that movement is the functional link between the subjective and objective components of human understanding. Perhaps then it is fitting to close our discussion by retelling his familiar story of the cave dwellers. In this analogy, you will remember, the prisoners were bound hand and foot at birth and confined within a deep cavern. Outside the cave were all the objective realities of the world of men, but the prisoners knew nothing of them. Confined within the cave, they knew only the shadows that flickered on the walls, and they knew themselves only as a vague sensation of being that was indistinguishable from the shadows.

In time, the prisoners were released from their chains and compelled to stand up, turn their heads toward the light, and move out of the cave into the outer realm of reality. As they did this, they discovered the relationship between the shadows and the objective forms which cast them, and they discovered their own relationship to these inner and outer realities of their own lives.

Only by moving themselves could the prisoners discover the objective forms of reality; only by pushing, pulling, tugging, squeezing, and manipulating the material forms of reality could they shape them into new forms which represented their own ideas—forms which could be perceived by other men within the subjective caverns of their own awareness. And so they moved about, sorting out the forms they observed, speculating about the SFRs which gave those forms their identity, developing hypotheses about the organization of reality, conceiving of new ways in which it might be reorganized, and verifying those hypotheses by manipulating the materials of the world into new forms.

CHAPTER 3

MAN-MADE MOVEMENT FORMS

...an abstraction given head,
A giant on the horizon, given arms,
A massive body and long legs
stretched out...
Imposing forms they can not describe,
Requiring order beyond their speech.

As Ug and his cave mates discovered within themselves the ability to create new forms, they formulated their emerging ideas in many different kinds of materials. Using the power of their own muscles to implement their ideas, they shaped air into recognizable word sounds, wood and stone into tools, bright pigments into pictures, and lumps of clay into representations of themselves and their gods. And at times they used themselves as materials, giving substantial form to their ideas by creating dynamic patterns of movement which served to communicate those ideas to their companions.

The earliest of these man-made movement forms were probably shaped as gestures. A circular movement of one arm, for example, might be used to denote the idea of *come* or *come toward me*; and perhaps a turning of the head from side to side denoted the idea of reluctance to move in the direction indicated by the beckoner. Either gesture might be performed slowly and cautiously, or it might be executed quickly and repeatedly. These variations in the general pattern of the gesture served to connote certain ideas about the feelings and emotional state of the mover. Thus, the gesture form symbolized the mover's interest in the event or how he felt about it or what it meant to him, as well as the primary idea it denoted.

Out of these powerful and confusing gesture symbols, they gradually developed the more complex patterns of movement known as dance. To give the first maker of dances a name, let us call him Kor.

We do not know what ideas Kor dealt with in his earliest dances, but we may speculate that they had something to do with his feelings about the forces which seemed to govern and control his life. From early paintings and clay figures, we may assume that he had some vague and often confused conception of a power which controlled the natural events of his world. This power could make his life good; it could send sun, rain, water, food, warmth, and security. It could also destroy his life; it could withhold the rain, dry up the water hole, wither the grasses, freeze the air, and cause him to suffer and die. Kor did not know what this power was nor where it had its dwelling place, but like most primitive people, and many of their descendants, he conceived of it as "above" him, above the sun and the rain, somewhere in the far reaches of the sky.

As he stood looking toward the sky, trying to comprehend this power, Kor's feelings were confused and ambivalent. At times he was so overwhelmed by awareness of its omnipotence that he prostrated himself before it, or perhaps he indicated his submission by bowing his head. At other times, he tried to persuade this power with gestures of supplication, raising his hands toward the sky to beckon its forces downward in the service of his needs. At other times he made a very different gesture—a gesture of defiance. Then he shook his fist at the sky, calling attention to his own powers and his intent to use them to overcome the forces of nature.

All these gestures denoted some idea about Kor's relationship to the powers "above" him, and all connoted some sense of his feelings and emotions as he considered that relationship. Out of these gestures, he fashioned the first dance forms.

The gestures had been spontaneous expressions of his confused ideas and feelings. Now he sought to clarify their patterns and explore their connotational properties. Perhaps he began by exaggerating each part of the complex movement pattern. Drawing himself up to his full height, he turned his face toward the sky, bending his neck backward, arching his back, and perhaps lifting his arms with his hands reaching upward as if to feel the power above him. Then, slowly, deliberately, he began his "act of submission," bringing his arms down and in toward his body, bending his neck, shoulders, elbows, back, and knees as he sank toward the earth, prostrating himself in a posture of helplessness.

The connotations Kor found in these movement patterns intensified and clarified his own complex feelings about this unknown power. Exploring ways of making these patterns apparent to other members of the tribe, he experimented with raising his arms, now this way, now that. He called attention to one arm pattern by holding it for a second or two, perhaps moving his fingers to direct attention to this position. He worked out configurational relationships, such as: How shall I stand as I raise my arms? What shall I do with my feet? When shall I rise to my toes to emphasize the upward reaching? In what order will I flex my body segments as I sink down into the posture of submission? He worked out time relationships, such as: How long shall I hold my arms out in the posture of supplication? What time pattern shall I create by moving my feet, my arms, my head? He worked out space relationships, such as:

How far shall I stretch out my arm? Can I make this movement larger? Should I make it smaller? Can I make it seem larger or smaller than it is by directing attention to it or by diverting attention from it? How are the movements of my head, arms, legs, and feet related to each other within the overall pattern of the form?

Probably Kor danced his own dance form as he presented it to the tribe, even as many choreographers do today, but we may denote the distinction between devising dance forms and performing them by giving the dancer a distinguishing name. Let us call him Dan.

As Dan performed the patterned and stylized movements which had been devised by Kor, he was not expressing his own feelings in spontaneous gestures. Rather, he was deliberately constructing a dynamic form which might serve to connote certain ideas, feelings, and emotions which had been explored by Kor. Then, as the other members of the tribe recognized these dynamic patterns, they found many connotations in them. These were not necessarily the same ideas, feelings, and emotions Kor had found in the dance. But to the extent that recognition of the patterns of the dance evoked *any* ideas, feelings, and emotions in the watchers, the dance was meaningful to them.

Kor also stylized the fist-shaking movement pattern, which evoked a different conception of man's relationship to the powers above him. Here, too, he enlarged the movement pattern, exaggerated parts of it, selected subpatterns within it; he arranged and organized the subpatterns, timed them, repeated some of them, and organized them into a sequence called a *war dance* or a *hunting dance*. These dances evoked a conception of man's own powers. They suggested such ideas as I am powerful, I am brave, I can kill my enemy, I can kill the dangerous beast. As men danced these dances together in a circle which symbolized their solidarity as a group of men, their courage grew within them, their fears were subdued, and they went forth to battle or hunt believing in themselves and their own powers.

Probably these first dances were little more than exaggerated and stylized presentations of familiar gestures and movements which denoted a specific act or action. But in time certain subpatterns of movement within the dance sequences became meaningful in their own right. Perhaps a pattern made by the feet, or a twist of the body as the dancer moved from one position to another, was so often repeated that doing these movements, or seeing them, was sufficient to suggest the whole dance, the conceptions connoted by it, and the feelings and emotions evoked by those conceptions. When this happened, a stylized subpattern might be used to symbolize all the ideas, feelings, and emotions formerly identified with the whole dance, and a new dance might evolve from a series of these subpatterns.

These new dances evoked the old ideas, feelings, and emotions and sometimes acquired new connotations of their own; some of them became meaningful in their own right long after the original sources of the movement patterns had been forgotten. Thus, each tribe developed characteristic dance forms and found them meaningful as formulations of ideas, feelings, and emotions; but seldom did two different tribes find the same meanings in each other's dances.

In time, some of these dances acquired a very special meaning as symbols of magical power. For example, if a rain dance was followed by a downpour, the dance was credited with power over the forces of nature. Then it seemed important to preserve the magic of the dance by doing it in precisely the same way every time it was performed, down to the smallest detail and nuance of the movement patterns. Three stamps of the right foot, three stamps of the left foot, one fist shake to the right at precisely shoulder height, a similar fist shake to the left, three head turns, and two hops—these details within the movement sequence were kept intact to preserve the magic in the dance form, even though they had no innate significance in the original formulation of the dance.

Thus, certain movement patterns were ritualized without reference to their original significance. These movements seemed meaningless to the members of other tribes who knew nothing of their derivation, but such ritualistic movements were of the utmost significance to the initiated, because for them the pattern evoked a sense of magical power, which transcended the limits of human power and human understanding.

Thus Kor and Dan discovered that men could give form to their emerging ideas, feelings, and emotions by shaping their own movements into dynamic patterns, but they did not exhaust the possibilities of formulating meanings by moving. Across the clearing their companion Ath was preoccupied with a different idea and a different way of formulating it in his own movements.

In full view of his companions, Ath picked up a long stick and hurled it into space. He threw it in much the same way he might throw a spear at an animal in the hunt, but now there was no animal in the clearing. Having thrown his stick at nothing, Ath then walked to where it had fallen, picked it up, and carried it back to the starting point. He stood there for a moment, hefting the stick in his hands and wriggling his shoulders about, and then he gathered all his forces together and again threw the stick at nothing.

To some of Ath's companions, the whole performance seemed absurd, and they shook their heads over this waste of time and energy. Others found it interesting; and soon another hunter picked up his own spear and hurled it into the clearing, where it fell short of Ath's farthest mark.

Did the second hunter miss the mark because he was a poor thrower? Or was it because his spear was heavier than Ath's stick? Or because he was standing behind Ath when he threw? Or had he been distracted by the sight of Ath jumping out of the way? Or by the possibility that Ug might throw a clay pot at him?

So Ath and his fellow athlete drew a starting line on the ground; they found two sticks which were of the same length, circumference, and weight; they agreed on no running, toes behind the line, and one hand only. They agreed that the throw counted only if the stick fell within certain boundaries, and they agreed to take turns and not hamper each other. Then they threw their sticks with all their might and marked the points where they fell.

As they compared the distances represented by these marks, neither could raise any questions about the circumstances which might have influenced them. Now, clearly, the farther mark represented the better throw. Or, we may say that the distance was an objective measure of the athlete's ability as a thrower of sticks. To the extent that this throw represented the athlete's work as a hunter, this measure of distance might also seem to connote a conception of Ath's skill in hunting.

But we must not press this interpretation further, for we have already pushed the evidence of human history too far in assuming that Ath could deal with the concept of objectivity and the concept of man-made rules. We must turn to the much later story of some funeral games held only three thousand years ago and described by Homer in the *Iliad*.

Patroclus, you will recall, was a noble Greek warrior who traced his ancestry to the gods. In life, he did all that the gods might expect of such a man. At his funeral, his noble companions sought to remind the gods of "the excellence of Patroclus" by competing in a track meet.

The events in this track meet represented actions which a noble warrior might be expected to perform many times in the heat of battle. For obituary use, they were extracted from the confusion of war and displayed within a set of rules, which defined them as javelin throwing, discus hurling, wrestling, foot racing, and chariot racing.

Perhaps we would like to think that this was a solemn occasion, but, alas, the whole affair was marred by angry quarrels, charges, and countercharges among the competitors in each event. These arguments were not about the scores that denoted how far the javelins traveled or about who had come in first in the races. Rather, they were all about wily and devious attempts to gain some personal advantage over other competitors.

Such wily and devious strategies were commonplace on the battlefield. Like every nobleman worthy of the name, Patroclus had gloried in his ability to devise and use such tactics, and the very gods, themselves, were noted for deceit and trickery. But now, in the funeral demonstration of the virtues of Patroclus, the men who used such strategies were accused of cheating.

This accusation went far beyond the refusal to recognize their marks by awarding them the prizes Achilles had provided for the first- and second-place winners. In each accusation, the larger conception of the man's honor as a nobleman was at stake, and each accused man fought to clear his honor rather than to obtain the prize that represented it.

And so it has been from that day to this. The scores we earn in sport tell little about how well we "throw our sticks" within the complexities of our lives, when our actions are governed by necessity or considerations of material value. Sport scores denote only how well we threw the stick under a very special set of conditions, specified by us. The rules that define those conditions permit us to compare our scores with the scores of other men; they also demand that we conduct ourselves in accordance with the highest standards of human behavior.

Perhaps Ath understood this in his own wordless way. Perhaps not. Perhaps the rough Greek warriors scarcely recognized the import of their own hastily made rules or the source of their anger at those who treated these rules lightly. Nonetheless, as they sought to portray the excellence of Patroclus, they formulated the dual conceptions of his *prowess* and his *honor* in the terms of sport.

The earliest forms of dance were created by men who had no words to describe them. The earliest sport forms were created by men who left few written records of their own history.

But the forms called exercise are of much more recent origin. They had to await many discoveries about the structure and functions of the human body; we shall defer our analysis of these important forms to a later chapter.

Here, we may content ourselves with a summary statement about the common characteristics of all man-made movement forms. All may be described as a coherent organization of movements designed to give material form to an idea; all have the properties of symbols, in that they are subject to three different modes of interpretation. As we perform or observe these man-made movement forms, we may ask Sci's questions: What materials are involved? How are those materials organized? Or we may ask Ven's questions: What idea is denoted by this dynamic form? What function does it serve? Or we may ask Pat's question: What ideas, feelings, and emotions are connoted by the dynamic patterns men create by moving? And with Fil we may recognize that all three questions are important to our understanding of the meanings we find in man-made movement forms, even though we may sometimes find it difficult to express that understanding in the verbal forms called *words*.

CHAPTER 4

SOURCES OF MEANING IN MOVEMENT

What we know in what we see,
what we feel in what
We hear,
What we are . . .
And what we think . . .

As Ug moved about in his small world, perceiving its natural forms, speculating about how they were organized, hypothesizing about how they might be reorganized, and verifying those hypotheses by shaping the materials of the world into new forms, he seldom thought about his own movements. Nonetheless, every movement he made provided him with new sources of meaning.

Lying motionless inside his cave, he could see its walls and the shadows that flickered across them, he could perceive the heat of the cave and its many odors, he could hear the roar of thunder and the cries of the animals in the forest, and he could taste the dryness in his own throat. But that was all he could know about how reality was organized, how its many forms functioned, and how he might function as a human form of life.

As he moved out of the cave, every step he took made new perceptions available to him, and he was able to abstract from them many conceptions about the functional organization of reality. In this way, he found the meaning of many concepts which he later called by such names as size, weight, big, little, heavy, light, gravity, inertia, mass, speed, rhythm, force, resistance, tension, fatigue, and muscle contraction.

Nonetheless, he seldom thought about his own movements; and as he sat under the tree wrestling with his emerging conception of a portable water container, he was not aware that his hands were moving in all directions. Neither was he aware of the patterns of movement in his fingers as he picked up a blob of clay, squeezed it, rolled it around in his hand, and then tossed it away. But by moving in this way, he learned more about his ability to overcome the inertia of the forces that binds particles of clay together.

Ug did not try to analyze the meanings he found in this clay-squeezing experience. Rather, he incorporated his conception of it into his emerging conception of a portable water container, and suddenly he seemed to understand what he was thinking about. He picked up another blob of clay, and movement by movement he overcame its inertial resistance and imposed his own conception of a set of SFRs upon it. When he had finished his self-conceived and self-chosen task, he found that he had created a new form of reality which was meaningful to him in many ways. He had also demonstrated that he could bend the forces of the universe to his will by moving in ways of his own choosing.

As Ug pushed, pulled, patted and squeezed the clay, each finger traced its own dynamic pattern in space, but Ug was not interested in the SFRs within these patterned movements. He was interested only in the effect those movements had on the clay. However, he soon observed that some of these movements were more effective than others, and gradually he sorted out the patterns of these effective movements and made a deliberate attempt to execute them precisely. Or we may say that these movements were meaningful to him as the functional link between his subjective idea about how the clay might be reorganized and his objective formulation of that idea. Soon he was able to objectify his understanding of the properties of those movements whenever he needed those precise movements in his work.

In general, Ug, Sci, Ven, Pat, and Fil were also interested in the effect their movements had on their materials, rather than in the movements that produced that effect. But Kor, Dan, and Ath were not able to make this distinction. The "blobs of clay" they were reorganizing were their own human bodies, and they were imposing their conceptions of possible sets of SFRs on their own movements.

As they formulated these conceptions by moving their own bodies, each man played a dual role. He was the perceiver; he was also the material being perceived. He was the thinker; he was also the organization of material he was thinking about. He was the mover; he was also the clay being shaped by those movements. And he could not wholly distinguish his own movements from the effect they had on the "blob of clay," because the effect produced was the very movement he used to produce it. Or, we might say that the movers and their conceptions of movement were both the subject and the object of their own interest. Within these dual roles, they found many sources of meaning that were not available to the makers of clay forms.

Ug could perceive how the clay was being reorganized by the effects of his movements, but he could not know how the clay experienced this reorganizing process. In their dual roles as movers and materials being moved, Kor, Dan, and Ath could experience this reorganizing process as it occurred within their own bodies. Externally, each could perceive the changing configuration of his own body, the patterns it traced in space, and the effect its movements had on other material forms. Internally, each could perceive both the pattern of his own movements and the effect those movements had on his own body. Each could perceive a pattern of kinesthetic, tactile, and visceral sensations and could also be aware of how he felt about the experience of moving in this way.

Within the process of performing his organization of movements, any of these conceptions might have been meaningful to him. He might also have found other meanings in any pattern he perceived within the performance situation. But he did not have time to think about these conceptions while he was performing. Rather, he had to comprehend these patterns as he recognized them, and incorporate his conceptions of them into the organization of movements instantaneously. Nonetheless, this often vague feedback of information about the effects his movements had on him served to clarify his conception of what he was trying to do, and he used it to modify his movement patterns even while he was performing them. Later, he also used this meaningful information to clarify his conception of the form before he made a second attempt to perform it.

In time, Ath became very skillful in stick throwing, and he no longer needed to think about the details of his movements as he performed them. But he still tried to recall those internalized patterns before he threw, hefting his stick and rehearsing the coordinations he was about to perform.

In time, too, Dan knew his dances so well that he could perform them more or less mechanically. But when he wanted to give his best performance, he had to focus his attention on the internal dynamics of his movement patterns in order to execute them exactly as Kor had designed them. Probably he thought about these internalized patterns more often than Ath did, because his movements served no purpose other than that of performing those patterns.

The men who watched Dan and Ath perform also had to recognize the dynamic patterns of the form as they occurred, because each pattern was being destroyed even while it was being created. In this sense, the spectators had only one conception of the movement form—a rather blurred conception of an ever-changing series of dynamic patterns made by a man as he moved about in space; and whatever meanings they found in the movement form had to be found in this one glimpse of it. In contrast, the men who saw, touched, handled, carried, filled, and drank from Ug's bowl had many opportunities to develop new conceptions of its SFRs. To them, it was a useful object, which might have been made by anyone, and they had no reason for identifying Ug with the patterns they found in it. Or, we may say that they could be wholly objective in dealing with their conceptions of the bowl.

But they could not touch, handle, carry, or use the movement forms in any way; they saw them only once and could not separate them from their conceptions of the persons who performed them. In this sense, their understanding of these forms was derived from wholly subjective sources; these sources were highly personalized, because they could not avoid identifying a conception of person, as well as a conception of dynamic movement patterns. Accordingly, it was easy for them to identify themselves with the persons who performed the movements; many of the meanings they found in their conceptions of the movement forms reflected their own conceptions of themselves as persons.

Within this transient, personalized, empathetic context, however, the sources of meaning in movement forms are identical with the sources of meaning in any other kind of material form. Whatever may be recognized within the form or within the situation in which the form is perceived may be a source of meaning. Conceptions may be abstracted from visual perceptions, from auditory perceptions, and from perceptions of touch, odor, or taste. They may also be abstracted from awareness of one's own feelings and emotions.

Incidentally, it may be noted that the kinesthetic perceptions which we may identify with our recognition of a movement form performed by another person are not perceptions of *his* sensations. Rather, we experience these sensations within ourselves. Such sensations can only be elicited by the pressures, pulls, and tensions of our own muscle contractions or by the effect of our own movements.

If we do experience such sensations while watching a performance, as many people do, we may account for them in two ways. At times our interest in the details of the movement patterns we are recognizing is so intense that it prompts us to try to reproduce those patterns. Then we seem to construct a miniature replica of the observed patterns by contracting our own muscles or by increasing the tension in the muscles which would be most involved in creating such a pattern. This tension change serves to stimulate the proprioceptor nerve endings, and we experience the kinesthetic sensations elicited by those miniature contractions.

It is also conceivable that our recognition of certain familiar movement patterns may evoke a conception of the kinesthetic sensations we have previously experienced as we performed them. Such a conception might be likened to thinking about a sound which had once been heard and is now recalled. In this case, there is no necessity for postulating overt muscle contractions which might stimulate the proprioceptors directly, because we are dealing with a conception of sensation rather than the immediate perception of the sensation, as such. However, this conception, which is evoked or connoted by some other recognition, may also prompt us to move in the patterns it denotes. If this happens, these actual changes in the tension of the muscles may elicit new kinesthetic sensations, which may be perceived directly.

Summarizing all these observations about the sources of meaning available to the performer and those available to an observer, we may note that all man-made forms of movement, however they may be perceived, may function as symbolic forms, characterized by the properties of being, denotation, and connotation. In substantive terms, these forms may be described as organizations of bodily movements or as a dynamic organization of a person within the context of a certain situation. However we may describe them, these movement forms denote some idea or conception of what the person is doing or trying to do. They also serve to evoke other ideas, feelings, and emotions which are connoted rather than denoted by our recognition of certain patterns within the form.

As we proceed with our analysis of the special properties of the movement forms called *dance, sport, exercise,* and *education,* we need not rehearse the properties of being, because these are virtually the same for all man-made forms of movement. The distinctions among the several forms arise at the level of denotation, as indicated by the need for giving each form a distinctive name. We shall begin our analysis of each form by trying to identify the kinds of ideas which seem to be denoted by it and then speculate about the kinds of ideas, feelings, and emotions which might be evoked as connotations.

Within this analysis, we shall need to distinguish between the sources of meaning available to the performer and those available to other persons who observe the form as spectators. To maintain this distinction, we shall use the term *performance* to denote the idea of the performer's involvement in the form. In contrast, when we approach our analysis from the observer's point of view, we shall call it a *presentational form.*

CHAPTER 5

DANCE FORMS

... a breathing like the wind,
A moving part of a motion ...
... a flow of meanings with no speech,
And of as many meanings as of men.

A dance form is an organization of movement patterns.

The conception of these patterns is denoted in the description of the dance; the performance of the dance also denotes this conception.

Other conceptions may be connoted by the patterns of the dance as a whole, or by the SFRs of any recognizable patterns within it.

In general, these connoted conceptions are potentially more interesting than the actual patterns of the dance.

As a dancer moves about in space, his personal relationships with the space around him will be changed in many obvious and subtle ways. These changes may be perceived as dynamic patterns, and the dance as a whole may be recognized as a complex composition of such patterns. The name we assign to such a complex composition, perhaps *waltz*, *frug*, or *Swan Lake*, also denotes the conception of these dynamic patterns.

These patterns may be defined or described in various ways. We may denote our conception of them with words like *step-step-close*, or *twist*, or *tour jeté* or by arranging little circles, squares, and arrows on a sheet of paper to indicate the force, direction, and size of the movements to be performed with each body part. Or we may denote our conception of these patterns by moving our own bodies in appropriate ways.

In whatever way we define or denote these dynamic patterns, they are still very much like the designs we might make by twirling an object in space or by arranging matchsticks on a blotter. In themselves, such designs are virtually meaningless. They become meaningful only as they serve to evoke some conception-idea-concept, feeling, or emotion, which is connoted, rather than denoted, by the intricate patterns we recognize in the design. The patterns we perceive in a dance also can evoke or connote certain meaningful conceptions, feelings, and emotions. The primary purpose of dancing is to evoke such connotational meanings.

However, the dancer does not necessarily recognize this purpose as he enters into the dance. Paradoxically, he may defeat this purpose by trying to analyze and define the connotations he finds interesting and meaningful. But if we wish to understand the purposes served by all dance forms and the ways in which those purposes are achieved, we must take this paradoxical risk.

The name we give to a dance denotes our conception of its identity as a specific composition of dynamic patterns. When we perform a dance of that name, we try to bring these patterns into being by moving in appropriate ways. Apparently our efforts serve no purpose other than that of bringing these patterns into being. In this sense, we may say that we dance to formulate or denote our conception of certain dynamic patterns—only this, and nothing more.

Nonetheless, the meanings we find in dancing a dance or in seeing it performed are not denoted by these recognizable patterns. Rather, we find those meanings in the connotations the patterns may have for us. Or we may say that these meanings are evoked by our personal interpretation of those patterns. We cannot ask the denotational questions: What does this dance mean? What is the idea in this dance? What is this dance about? What conceptions, feelings, and emotions are denoted by it? What am I supposed to think and feel as I perform this dance or see it performed?

If these meanings could be neatly pinned down and defined with denotational words, there would be little reason for trying to evoke some conception of them by performing the complex movements of a dance. Rather, we might better explain those meanings by saying: Here is an idea. Here is how I feel about it. Here is what I think other people feel about it.

When we try to explain the meanings we find in the connotations of a dance, we are, in effect, trying to write a definitive essay. Every word we use seems to denote the idea that the meanings we find in a dance can be defined, denoted, and verbalized. We must remind ourselves again and again that a dance does not *denote* any idea other than a conception of a composition of dynamic patterns which may be brought into being by the movements of a person. This composition is brought into being for the purpose of evoking whatever connotations each person may find in his own relationship with the dance.

The choreographer who develops the original conception of a dance composition must have at least an intuitive understanding of this connotation-evoking purpose and the ways in which this purpose may be achieved. This understanding should be shared by the dancer, who brings this composition into being on a stage so that its patterns may be perceived by an audience. Both the choreographer and the dancer will be able to use this understanding more effectively if they analyze and define it. But the viewers in an audience and the people who dance for their own enjoyment do not need to analyze this purpose in order to achieve it. Rather, they may find their own involvement in the dance more meaningful if they let the dance serve this connotation-evoking purpose in its own nonverbal way.

As the choreographer attempts to create a composition of dynamic patterns which will serve to evoke meaningful connotations, he begins with some conception of a movement pattern. We might call this conception an idea of a pattern, but this would suggest a clearly structured conception of the SFRs within the movement; this would be misleading, because the choreographer does not yet have this much understanding of these SFRs. His initial conception of the movement pattern is a vaguely defined recognition of some change in the relationships between a person and his surroundings.

Having found his initial conception of such a pattern, he then begins to explore the SFRs within it by expanding it, contracting it, distorting it, emphasizing certain elements in it, and combining it with other patterns. He also explores the connotational properties of the pattern by asking: Why do I find this pattern interesting? What connotations are evoked by my recognition of this pattern? He may not be able to define these connotations, and usually he cannot, but he must still try to clarify his own recognition of them, because every decision he makes about the structure of the movement patterns to be used in the dance will rest on some conception of their connotational function.

The criterion he uses to judge the "rightness" or "wrongness" of each pattern within the composition is some conception of the connotations it evokes for him, but he must not let himself fall into the paradoxical trap of trying to denote those connotations. If he does, he will defeat his own purpose, which is to compose patterns evoking meanings which cannot be denoted in any definitive form. Unfortunately, many choreographers do fall into this trap, and we know that this has happened whenever we see a dance which clearly represents an idea which can be fully explained in words. Strictly speaking, this acting out of an idea cannot be called a dance, because it does not do what a dance does.

Working back and forth between his conception of the SFRs within the interesting movement patterns and his own conception of their connotational properties, the choreographer designs his composition of dynamic patterns. This composition may eventually evoke for other people some of the connotations it has for him, or it may not. It will accomplish the purposes for which it was designed if it evokes *any* connotations which are meaningful to the people who perform the dance or see it performed.

One long-ago choreographer probably discovered his initial conception of certain person-space relationships in the actions of a child who was taking a bath in a round tin tub filled with very hot water. We do not know that this was the source of his conception, but we can infer this from our own recognition of the person-space relationships in the dance. This inference is strengthened by the composer's reference to "Saturday night" in the song which both describes the movements of the dance and accompanies them.

The words of this song are: "I put my little hand in; I pull my little hand out; I give myself a shake, shake, shake; and turn myself about. Here we go looby-loo, here we go looby-light, here we go looby-loo, all on a Saturday night." Then, the other hand, each foot, and finally "my whole self" are put in, pulled out, and shaken in the interests of doing the patterns of looby-loo.

The movement patterns of looby-loo resemble the movements a child of long ago might have made in taking a bath, but they do not denote either this action or this purpose, because they obviously do not serve this purpose. Rather, they serve the purposes of dancing; and apparently they have served those purposes very well, because they have been danced willingly and with enjoyment by thousands, yes, millions of children who did not identify them with bathing.

We do not know what connotations these children found in their recognition and performance of these movement patterns. If we were to ask them, they probably could not tell us, because they did not analyze them or try to explain them in words. But we can speculate about those connotations by asking ourselves what kinds of ideas, feelings, and emotions they suggest to us.

To me, the movement patterns of reaching out, withdrawing, shaking, and turning suggest a conception of the conflicting feelings inherent in the process of "growing up to be a man." I think the dance is meaningful to children who are experiencing these conflicting feelings because it evokes a conception of them which can be experienced and explored without running the risks inherent in the actual growing-up process.

"Growing up to be a man" can be an exciting, frightening, and rewarding process at any age. It was an intensely fearsome experience for the boys who came to manhood during the years of World War II, an experience made more complex by the need to hide those fears. To me, the sense of these complex feelings is connoted by the adult wartime version of looby-loo, which was called the hokey-pokey.

In the hokey-pokey, the old tune was "jazzed up" and the dancers moved to a syncopated beat. The hand became a fist, with pointing index finger, and every movement in the dance was enlarged and executed forcefully. The old words were changed to fit these forceful and syncopated movements, with the emphasis falling on the italicized words. "I put my *right* arm in" was executed in stride position with a full striking pattern as the fist with its extended index finger was snapped into place, pointing toward the center of the circle. "I pull my *right* arm out" reversed this pattern. "I *do* the hokey-pokey as I *shake* it all about." Here "it" referred to a very important part of the body which could not be named directly but was shaken vigorously as the extended finger was raised overhead and waggled from side to side. Then the dancers shuffled or "trucked" around the circle, waggling their fingers overhead, doing the hokey-pokey. Left arm, right leg, and left leg were successively put in and pulled out, and finally "all of me" was committed to the requirements of the dance.

Did these fearful and brave young men who were growing up in a hokey-pokey world of danger and death recognize the connotations of the movement patterns of reaching out, withdrawing, and shaking? Did they identify the pointing finger as a symbolic gun or as a phallic symbol? Did they sense the connotations of bravado in the finger-waggling pattern? Did they comprehend the sense of assurance with which they resolved their in-out-shake conflicts by resolutely shuffling along or "trucking on down?" Probably not. Probably they would have been embarrassed beyond words if anyone had suggested such meanings to them. But we do know that they called for this adult version of an old children's dance again and again, not just because the movement patterns could be performed with any "hello–good-bye" partner in the USO recreation centers, but because the feelings and emotions evoked by this performance were meaningful to them.

Looby-loo and the hokey-pokey are participational forms of dance. The characteristic movement patterns are experienced by the people who dance them and are designed to serve their interests. They may also be recognized by someone who sees them danced, but such recognition is only incidental to the concerns of the participants.

When a child or young soldier is fully involved in the process of doing a dance, he is not thinking about how it looks or about the meanings an observer may find in it. If he does entertain such thoughts while he is dancing, he becomes self-conscious. The sense of being watched and evaluated may inhibit his movements, or it may motivate him to extend and amplify them for the benefit of the audience. In either case, his attention is diverted from his personal involvement in the meanings of the dance and directed toward some conception of how the dance looks or how it is visualized by someone else.

In composing a presentational dance form, this is precisely what the choreographer does think about. Now the purpose of the composition is to evoke ideas, feelings, and emotions which will be meaningful to those who perceive the dance as a visual form. Accordingly, the choreographer starts with some conception of a visibly perceivable pattern.

Let us assume that he finds his initial conception in what he sees as he watches a performance of one of the participational dances which were meaningful to the people of Israel while they were attempting to establish a new nation and an old religion in an arid and hostile land.

One formation used in many of these national dances is called *the circle of solidarity*. In this formation, the dancers stand very close together with their arms across the shoulders of the dancers on either side. In this tightly interlocked circle, they move with small, easy steps, either turning slightly sideward to run around the circle or moving sideward by crossing one foot in front or in back of the other. Usually the circle moves clockwise for a few steps, then counterclockwise, so each dancer maintains his own place on the rim as the circle of solidarity moves back and forth around the center.

The feelings and emotions which can be generated by repeating these interlocking steps in such a circle of solidarity have been experienced and valued by many people, both in and outside of Israel. To some extent, these same feelings and emotions may be evoked by seeing these dances performed, but the watcher's interest may wane very quickly because he sees only a blurred image of these movement patterns, and he may find the continuous repetition of that image monotonous. However, the choreographer may find this blurred image sufficiently interesting to warrant further investigation. If he does, he will begin to explore and try to clarify the patterns he has perceived within it; and in order to make the SFRs within those patterns more clearly visible, he will experiment by exaggerating and emphasizing every pattern.

Perhaps he begins his composition with one dancer. He visualizes him moving slowly across the stage, reaching toward the center. This dancer is followed by other dancers in scattered formation, all pointing and reaching. As they move about, their paths intersect, and they bump into each other, and one by one they fall to the ground in a jumble of bodies with others scattered around. Then one dancer emerges from the heap by rising to his knees, and another dancer places his hands on the shoulders of the kneeling figure and stands erect. Perhaps two dancers whose arms are interlocked get to their feet as a unit. Out of such interactions, the dancers find upright positions, some alone and others together. Gradually, they find their way into a circular formation, and in time the steps of all the dancers are interlocked as the circle moves around the spot in the center of the stage.

Now the dancers introduce many variations into the basic step pattern, leaping, jumping, stamping, and hopping as they progress around the circle. Or perhaps they extend the circle by moving away from each other until only the hands are touching. Then they draw closer to each other until the circle of solidarity is a solid wall of bodies, while the steps are so precisely coordinated in an interlocking pattern that the wall seems to move as a single force. With each step the tempo increases, and the dance ends with the wall moving faster and faster, until the viewer sees only a blur of movement around a central purpose.

This very obvious acting out of certain ideas can scarcely be called a dance. A group of children might produce such a composition in a very short time. We could probably find some connotations in its patterns, but it is unlikely that our understanding of those ideas would be expanded by this experience.

If the dance is to serve the choreographer's purpose, it must be more than a composition of movement patterns which denote such actions as pointing, walking, impeding, falling, rising, and supporting. Each pattern must be taken out of this denotational context and carefully restructured and redesigned for the purpose of projecting an image of the SFRs within these person-space interactions. The choreographer must do what all artists do: He must select, arrange, rearrange, organize, reorganize, combine, and recombine the elements in these patterns with a view to projecting a visible image which has the power of evoking meaningful connotations.

The techniques used by the choreographer may be suggested by such terms as *exaggeration, distortion, repetition,* and *contrast*; others are described in books devoted to an exposition of the choreographic process. Using these techniques, the choreographer takes every movement pattern out of its denotational form and reshapes and redefines it in some way which will make it serve the connotation-evoking purposes of the dance.

How does he know when his composition is finished? There is no way to tell. He stops working on it when he feels reasonably well satisfied with it or perhaps only when the curtain rises on some presentation of it.

To serve the purposes of such a presentation, the choreographer may also select music, costumes, and a stage setting which he thinks will enhance the connotation-evoking powers of the dance. He might suggest the Israeli origins of his circle-of-solidarity dance with a blue curtain or perhaps with some representation of the Star of David or a menorah, and he might reinforce this suggestion by using musical themes drawn from religious sources.

Such obvious connotational aids might enhance the connotational properties of the dance, but they may also endanger them. If the viewer thinks that these aids denote the idea of a particular setting or situation in which the dance is meaningful, he may try to force his recognition of the connotations of the dance into that particular setting or situation. In doing this, he may well miss many of the very meaningful connotations he might find in the dance as a larger image of man's interactions with the realities of his life.

When the choreographer's composition is completed, he turns it over to the dancer who will bring its patterns into being as a visual image which can be seen by the audience.

The dancer starts his work by trying to get a clear visual image of the choreographer's patterns. Then, like every artist, he selects, arranges, rearranges, organizes, and reorganizes his own material elements in an attempt to clarify the SFRs within the patterns he is presenting. The elements with which he works are his own movements, which must now be structured to make the SFRs within the visible designs more apparent.

Perhaps one of the patterns designed by the choreographer may be described as a leap into the air and a descent which produces a spiraling pattern as the body makes contact with the ground, coming to rest in a flat, circular heap. The dancer studies the SFRs within this conception of a visually perceivable pattern and then attempts to devise the coordinations which will make those SFRs most apparent to the audience. In doing this he does not try to leap or fall in a heap. If he actually did the actions denoted by those words, he would experience the painful sensations which might be connoted by these patterns. Instead, he tries to produce the visual image of this leaping-falling pattern in such a way that he has full control over his own muscular coordinations at every point in the pattern, so that he may lower his body to the floor as slowly or as rapidly as he chooses, while arranging every body segment with equal care.

The choreographer cannot tell the dancer how to do this. He designed the visual image, but he does not devise the coordinations which might project it. This is the dancer's responsibility and the dancer's art. The techniques of that art are as well known as those which serve the needs of artists working in other media, but here let us say only that the dancer does two quite different things. He devises the coordinations which will project a visual image to an audience, and then he performs those coordinations on the stage. If he does his first task well, some of the connotation-evoking SFRs within the choreographer's composition will be evident to the viewers; if he does his second task well, those SFRs will be clearly apparent.

The dancer's relationship to the connotational properties of the dance he performs is both subtle and complex, particularly if he has also choreographed the dance composition he is dancing, as many dancers do. In the role of the choreographer, he was well aware of the connotations he found in the SFRs of the visible image of the dance. In the role of the dancer, he may well be tempted to try to project those connotations to the audience. But if he succumbs to this temptation, he, too, has fallen into the paradoxical trap of trying to denote connotations. To avoid this trap, he must focus his attention wholly on the dancer's art of performing the intricate coordinations he has devised to expose the SFRs of a visual image to the audience, which is to say that he must think solely about the conception of pattern denoted by the dance.

Can he denote such a pattern without being affected by the connotations it may evoke? Probably not. But this is precisely what he must try to do while he is performing the dance before an audience; perhaps the ultimate measure of his art is found in his ability to achieve this almost impossible purpose.

Later, after the dance is done and he has left the stage, he may permit himself to experience the meanings connoted by the dance, particularly if he has succeeded in evoking some conception of those meanings in the audience. But many dancers do not, which is indeed fortunate, especially if they are performing a series of quite different dances in one concert.

Here we must repeat again that the viewer who sees the dance performed has no obligation to discover any particular meanings in the dance he sees. To him the dance may appear to be a meaningless composition of patterns, and nothing more; he may find the dance interesting without analyzing the connotations he finds in its patterns; or it may connote to him a set of ideas, feelings, and emotions quite different from those envisioned by the choreographer and the dancer. In dealing with patterns and designs, each man's connotations are his own, and no one else can say what those connotations are or what they should be. Therefore the dance viewer is under no obligation to find any particular set of meanings in any dance. He will find much greater enjoyment in going to dance concerts if he lets each dance do what every dance is designed to do— evoke whatever ideas, feelings, and emotions it may as a composition of dynamic patterns which denotes nothing more than a conception of that composition.

Any dance form may serve the purpose of evoking meaningful conceptions of man's interactions with the realities of his life, but not all dance forms are equally popular in any cultural period. As time goes on, and men change their conceptions of themselves and their own lives, old dances lose their popularity and become "period pieces" which evoke conceptions of a way of life which existed in the past; other dance forms are modified to suggest new conceptions of man and new ways of dealing with reality; and new dance forms evolve or are choreographed within the context of the life style of each new generation.

The minuet, for example, was popular with the landed gentry of the seventeenth and eighteenth centuries. It is seldom danced today, except perhaps on Washington's Birthday, when its historical significance is clearly indicated by dressing the women in crinolines and the men in brocade jackets with cascades of lace at the wrists. But the very thought of performing these graceful and stately movement patterns in blue jeans and sweatshirt is ludicrous.

American square-dance forms provide a particularly clear illustration of how a conception of a way of life may be connoted by the formations, figures, patterns, and terminology of a dance form. The basic formation is a square, reminiscent of the village squares of New England and the clearings around which the men and women of the westward trek built their homes. These "homes" are identified by name, and each home place is occupied by a couple. Every dance begins with some version of the commands: "honor your partner," "honor your neighbor," and "honor the company." Then, as each couple goes "howdy-ing around" to interact with the other couples, each man dances with every other woman in the set, not forgetting "old grand-maw" and including "the gal from Arkansaw." In some figures, the men come together in the square to create their own pat-terns of common effort; in other figures, the women gather in the square; and sometimes the call is "all hands around" for a common endeavor. But the final figure is always the same. The original partners meet, each couple "promenades home," and the dance ends with each man giving his lady a good-night "swing" in their own home place.

When these square-dance forms were danced in the vil-lages of New England, the steps of the dancers were light as they skipped to the pony-trot rhythm of Yankee Doodle. But as the heavy wagons rolled slowly over the Alleghenies, across the broad Missouri, into the Red River Valley, the light-footed skip gave way to a slow, steady shuffle which echoed the plodding rhythms of tired horses pulling heavy wagons over rough ground. Similarly, every other pattern in these dance forms changed in subtle or obvious ways which reflected some of the specific patterns in the life of each locale.

The connotations of these localized square-dance forms were intensely meaningful to the men and women who lived around squares and honored a strictly defined code of rules which governed their relationships with each other. They are much less meaningful to people who live in sprawling cities, ride in high-powered cars, and govern their conduct by a less strictly defined code. On occasion, we can be persuaded to dance modified versions of these old dance forms, particularly when wearing costumes reminiscent of an earlier day, but our interest in these historical conceptions is limited, and we do not understand their meanings as readily as we comprehend the feelings of our own time.

Conversely, it is almost impossible to imagine our ancestors moving in the patterns of the frug, which evokes a conception of a way of life and certain relationships between men and women which were virtually unthinkable a century ago.

This relationship between the connotations of a dance and the dancer's conception of his own way of life may also be seen in presentational and art forms, even as it has been traced in the changing styles of music, poetry, painting, and sculpture.

One interesting example of this relationship may be found in the precisely stylized movement patterns of the classical ballet. As the ballerina rises to the tip of one toe and whirls around on this almost invisible point of support, she is performing a very difficult feat which requires great strength and skill, but this is not what the audience sees. Rather, the visible pattern evokes a conception of an elegant and virtually effortless performance, in which the forces of the earth are overcome with ease and grace.

The classical ballet patterns were not devised for the delectation of heavy-footed peasants who worked the soil with the strength of their own backs and hands. They were devised to please the exalted personages of royalty and nobility, who believed that they were born to rule the earth without need for muscular effort, and the nobility never tired of seeing the dances which evoked this conception of an exalted, elegant, graceful way of life.

Swan Lake is still performed before appreciative audiences, but we may now recognize it as a "period piece," as a virtuoso performance, or as a fantasy. We may well enjoy this fantasy because it evokes one of our most enduring dreams of effortless living, but few of us expect to live this dream in the realities of our own lives.

The connotations that audiences found in the gossamer patterns of a scarf floating in the air may have had similar overtones, but perhaps these patterns can be better understood in the context of a period when artists in all media were preoccupied with various conceptions of the beauty of nature. The patterns of many of these "natural" dances were found in grasses waving in the wind, in daisies opening in the sun, or perhaps in Beethoven's conception of a pastoral scene. In their own time, these dances constituted a rebellion against the rigidly stylized patterns of the classical ballet, and dancers and audiences found this rebellion meaningful. Today, no dancer would dare to present these patterns to an audience for fear of inciting a riot of giggles.

Today, artists of every medium are experimenting with new techniques for evoking conceptions that are meaningful to men who are interacting with the realities of the universe in complex ways. Some are using representational techniques to compose forms which evoke their meanings in terms of some conception of a clearly recognizable interaction between man and the observable realities of his life. Others are using nonrepresentational, semiabstractional, and abstractional techniques to develop compositions which represent only the artist's conception of such a form. All these techniques are also being used by contemporary choreographers and dancers; some audiences find these compositions meaningful, while others do not. But this was ever so, in dance as in all other arts.

Styles in dance may come and go, even as men may change their styles of living and their ways of thinking about their lives, but within these changes the purposes of dancing are not changed. Today, as yesterday, dancers dance for two reasons. They dance to denote or formulate a conception of a sequence of dynamic patterns; they dance to evoke whatever connotations may be generated by awareness of the dynamic elements in those patterns. Some of the dynamic elements in their dances reflect their interest in other conceivable patterns that may be found in the scenes and events of their own time; some are born of their interest in the dynamic elements they find in their own attempts to move in consciously structured ways. Some of their dances are composed by choreographers who consciously select and arrange sequences of movements which they find interesting; some are developed, rather than composed, by untutored dancers who discover that certain sequences of movements are interesting to them. In general, the sequence of dynamic patterns that constitutes any one of these dances can be reasonably well described or diagramed in denotational words or other written symbols; the connotations the dancer finds in his performance of that sequence of dynamic patterns must be forever wordless. Nonetheless, the dancer's interest in dancing is predicated upon his interest in these wordless conceptions, feelings, and emotions. They constitute the primary source of whatever meanings he finds in the dance; knowingly or unknowingly, he finds the act of dancing meaningful because he finds those wordless connotations meaningful; and he dances for the purpose of evoking and experiencing the feelings and emotions that are evoked by those connotations.

CHAPTER 6

SPORT FORMS

I measure myself
Against a tall tree.
I find that I am much taller,
For I reach right up to the sun,
With my eye; . . .
Nevertheless, I dislike
The way the ants crawl
In and out of my shadow.

A sport form is an organization of effective actions.

The conception of these actions is denoted in a code of rules, and these rules also define the conception of "what counts" in evaluating the effectiveness of the actions.

The performance of the sport form denotes the conceptions set forth in the rules; it also serves to produce a score which denotes the conception of "what counts" in quantitative terms.*

Other conceptions may be connoted by the SFRs of the entire performance or by any recognizable set of SFRs within it.

---

* *In a few sport forms the performance may serve to kill an animal rather than to produce a quantitative score. This specialized category of sport forms is not considered in the ensuing discussion.*

*In general, the rules also recognize two distinctive classes of perform-
ers. An amateur performer must undertake to perform the sport with no
thought of necessity and no hope of material reward. A professional
performer may accept money or other material rewards for his performance or for his involvement with the sport form in some substantial
way, but having done so, he may not subsequently compete with
amateurs in officially organized performances.*

The list of sport forms that answer to this description is endless.
Within that list, each form has its own distinctive name, such as
baseball or skiing. It also has its own distinctive rules, its own
effective actions, its own meaningful vocabulary of terms, and
its own distinctive group of performers. Characteristically, these
performers take on the name of the sport, calling themselves
baseball players or skiers; they are seldom equally interested in
any other sport.

Or, we may say that baseball players find the meanings of
sport in such terms as *pitch, catch, strike, hit, run,* and *error,* but
characteristically, they find little or no meaning in the skier's
slaloms and *telemarken.* Similarly javelin throwers seldom play
tennis; sky divers rarely wrestle; few golfers own surfboards;
and so on through the endless list.

Within this diversity, however, every sport must also exhibit
certain meaningful characteristics that are common to all sport
forms. In order to find those sources of meaning, we must ignore
the distinctive differences among specific forms and ask: How
are all sport forms alike? How is baseball like skiing? How is
surfing like auto racing? How is wrestling like table tennis?
How is rugby like platform diving? How is gymnastics like bad-
minton? How is javelin throwing like sky diving? What do Olympic gold-medal winners and weekend golfers have in common?
That is, how is the definitive conception of sport exemplified in
all sport forms?

Every sport form may be described as an organization of
effective actions. As we survey any representative list of named
forms, it becomes apparent that these actions are directed

toward an attempt to make something move about in space. This "something" may be the performer's own body, as in skiing, gymnastics, high jumping, or sky diving. It may be the body of another person, as in boxing or wrestling. It may be an object, as in javelin throwing, tennis, or ice hockey. It may be a machine, as in auto racing or gliding. Or it may be an animal, as in dressage or calf roping.

To generalize these possibilities, we may say that the effective actions of the performer are directed toward an attempt to make some substantial organization of mass move about in space in some recognizable way. Or, we might say that the performer is attempting to overcome the inertial resistance of some organization of substantial materials.

During the performance, the performer may, in fact, overcome the inertia of his chosen materials many times, but his efforts have no permanent effect on them. When the performance is over, all the materials are still intact, and nothing has been changed by the performer's attempts to make them move through space in some recognizable way.

The athlete's javelin flies through space and falls to the ground; the distance is measured, and the javelin is brought back to the starting point or stored away unchanged. His skis carry him through the gates of the slalom course; then the gates are taken down, and the skier returns to his starting point. His ball is tossed into a bottomless basket, only to fall to the ground. His opponent rises from the mat and walks away, unharmed and undeterred. In this sense, we may say that the athlete performs the futile task of Sisyphus, whose name means "very wise" or "very clever."

In the time of Sisyphus, you will remember, the forces of the universe were controlled by the many gods who lived on Mt. Olympus. Sisyphus was only a mortal man, and his life was wholly controlled by those forces, but in his own clever way he discovered something about the organization of the universe that only the gods were supposed to know. When he used that knowledge to his own advantage, the gods had to punish him. And so they condemned him to spend all time and eternity performing the futile task of pushing a rock up a slope, in full knowledge of the fact that it would always roll back to the bottomless valley from whence it came, obliterating all trace of his mortal efforts.

All sport forms are governed by an elaborate code of rules in which every aspect of the task of Sisyphus is described, defined, and denoted in explicit terms. These rules also define what counts in evaluating the athlete's performance of this task.

In this code, every element of mass, space, and time that enters into the performer's conception of the task is clearly identified. The area in which the task is to be performed is described and perhaps diagramed, and all markings are clearly shown. The material characteristics and placement of any stationary equipment within that area are also denoted, and the characteristics of all implements and movable objects or devices are described in explicit terms. And, on occasion, the characteristics of the performers who may compete in any given event are listed in terms of sex, age, size, weight, and perhaps previous experience.

These rules also specify what the performer may and may not do within the sport arena. He may enter certain areas but not others. He may move his materials into the space above or within certain markings but not elsewhere.

The actions he may perform in dealing with these materials are also prescribed. He may strike the ball with one part of his racket but not with another. He may swing his stick so high or so far but no higher and no farther. He may throw, but not push, an object; he may propel it with his feet, but not with his hands, or conversely. He may collide with a moving object or person, but not with a stationary one. He may run on the third strike, under certain circumstances, but not on the second. (Etc., etc., etc., etc., etc.)

Furthermore, these rules prescribe how he should behave

while he is involved in the sport performance. This conception of sportsmanlike conduct is not always explicated in detail, but it is implicit within the general rules of sport and is interpreted in the same way in all sport forms.

The rules also prescribe the penalties that are to be assessed against any performer who does not obey them to the letter. These penalties may range from "loss of distance" to removal from the performance for repeated infractions of the rules; if it is later discovered that the performer did break certain rules while the performance was in process, the score he made may be declared null and void.

In all sports, the penalty for unsportsmanlike conduct is the same. If such conduct is exhibited during the performance, the performer is expelled from the area and denied the privilege of further participation in the sport event; if evidence of such conduct is found after the performance is finished, the score is declared invalid, and, on occasion, the performer may be barred from all further competition in sport.

In short, the rules that define a sport form specify every element of mass, space, time, action, and personal behavior which may be counted in the determination of the score. The only question left unanswered is: How well can the performer do what is prescribed by these rules?

The answer to that question is expressed in a quantitative score which denotes how far, how fast, how many times, or how precisely the performer or his team made the chosen organization of materials move through space in the prescribed way. Less obviously, but unquestionably, it must also denote the fact that the performer exemplified the conception of sportsmanlike conduct in his personal behavior while he was performing. Further, it usually connotes the fact that he has no professional or work-related interest in the effective actions of the sport.

Bringing all these observations together, we may describe a sport form as a self-chosen and rule-governed task which involves an attempt to overcome the inertia of certain substantial forms in certain specified ways; the performance of that task produces a conception of honorable behavior, a conception of the performance of the task, and a score which denotes the quality of that performance in quantitative terms.

In this sense, the performance seems to serve as a test of the performer's ability to accomplish a useless task. We may say that this is an objective test, because every material element in it was specially devised, designed, or reserved for this task, and no other, and each of these material elements can be duplicated in every subsequent performance of the test. Thus, the scores earned by different performers can be compared in meaningful ways, and each performer may interpret the scores he earns in many repetitions of the test in meaningful terms.

Nonetheless, the task used for this test is not only unnecessary, it is also trivial and futile. We may well wonder why the performer is so interested in obtaining many comparable measures of his ability to perform it. Or we may ask why the performer is so interested in testing and retesting his ability to toss a useless ball into a bottomless basket.

Perhaps we can partially explain his interest in this seemingly self-defeating experience by examining the differences between "life" and sport, rather than by considering their common features.

Life offers every performer many opportunities to test his own ability to overcome the inertia of mass. We cannot move without overcoming the inertia of our own body tissues; we cannot use the materials of the universe, or convert them into more usable forms, without imposing our own conceptions of a set of SFRs on them. But many conflicting considerations may enter into these demonstrations of our ability to overcome the inertia of the universe, and it is difficult, if not impossible, to define the conception of our own abilities in unequivocal terms.

In life, we must take our materials as we find them, soft or hard, light or heavy, elegant or shoddy, and we must do whatever may seem necessary to adapt them to our needs and the needs of other people. Often, we are not quite certain about what we are trying to do or why we must do it. At times, we are forced to work at a task that is not to our liking and not of our own choosing; usually we must consider the material value of our efforts and adapt our actions to the needs imposed by this conception. Also, other people may help, hinder, or coerce us in some way, and we cannot distinguish between the effects of their efforts and the effects of our own. So, too, our own interest in helping, hindering, or coercing other people may modify both our actions and our behavior. And while working at one task, either self-chosen or imposed, we are usually thinking of many other tasks that seem to demand our attention. In short, within the complex conditions of life, we are seldom, if ever, free to focus all our attention on one well-defined task and bring all the energies of our being to bear on one whole-hearted attempt to perform that task effectively.

In contrast, the rules of sport provide us with a man-made world in which this freedom is fully guaranteed. These rules eliminate the demands of necessity by defining an unnecessary task. They eliminate all need for consideration of material values by defining a futile task that produces nothing of material value. They eliminate all questions about the quality of materials by defining a set of materials of known quality. They eliminate all questions about what we are trying to do, and how we can best do it, by prescribing the actions that may be used to perform the task. They eliminate all doubt about what counts by describing how the performance of the task is to be evaluated. And they eliminate all need to debate our own motives and the motives of other people by imposing the same standards of conduct on all performers.

In this sense, the rules of sport provide each performer with a rare opportunity to concentrate all the energies of his being in one meaningful effort to perform a task of his own choosing, no longer pushed and pulled in a dozen directions by the many imperatives he may recognize in his life. Or, we may say that he may experience himself as a fully motivated, fully integrated, fully functioning human being.

As many performers have testified, this experience seems to re-create them, or restore their own sense of wholeness. And as a consequence of this experience, they are better able to cope with the divisive imperatives of life. Accordingly, they identify their interest in sport with this integrative experience, rather than with an interest in their own scores.

Other performers have testified that the physiological fatigue resulting from this integrative experience is qualitatively different from the fatigue produced by work in that it induces a feeling of well-being rather than a feeling of exhaustion. In this sense, many performers identify their interest in sport with its aftereffects, rather than with the scores they earn during the performance.

However, even though a performer may value recreation and a sense of well-being far more than he values his own score, he cannot shirk the task of making the best possible score while performing. The rules that permit him to achieve these integrative effects by focusing all his energies on one well-defined task also demand this score. If he does less, he is perverting the rules of sport and destroying the intrinsic pattern of the sport form—"throwing the game." Moreover, he is defeating his own interest in being integrated, because that feeling of wholeness is developed by focusing the wholeness of his being on the task of producing that score.

Summarizing our analysis of the differences between life and sport, it becomes apparent that the man-made rules which define a sport form also rule out all the considerations which may affect our behavior as we perform the real tasks of life. Equally, they rule out all the considerations that may influence our own interpretation of that behavior. Or we may say that the rules of sport impose a man-made set of SFRs upon the circumstances of our human existence.

In these man-made circumstances, no man can attribute

his successes or failures to any factor that lies beyond the boundaries of his own being. All his self-justifying excuses and pretenses are stripped away by the man-made rules he has devised and accepted; within those rules he is confronted with an image of himself, as he is, in the fullness of his own being, with whatever abilities he may have and with whatever talents he may have for using those abilities. Or, as the competitors in the early Olympic festivals put it, in the symbolic world of sport every man "stands naked before his gods." Stripped of all excuses, he must demonstrate his ability to perform a well-defined task of his own choosing; naked of all pretense, he must demonstrate his own talents for using those abilities under circumstances which permit him to function in the wholeness of his being as a fully integrated person.

Within this performance, he cannot delude himself about his own capabilities. He has voluntarily pledged himself to do his utmost in a symbolic world which permits and requires him to do and be the best of whatever he is able to do or be. In this symbolic world, he may find an image of himself at his best, and equally he may find an image of himself at his worst, but he cannot escape the implications of either image, because it is the image of himself at his utmost.

Neither can he escape his own feelings about that image as it is revealed to him within the performance. As he stands up to bat, with the bases loaded and two strikes against him, his feelings reflect his own interpretation of himself in this critical situation. And whatever he may feel, he has no time to sort out those feelings and debate about their rationale. He must experience them for what they are, and he must act in terms of those feelings even while he is experiencing them. Or we may say that he must actualize his own emotional patterns by acting in ways that demonstrate how he deals with them when he is functioning at his utmost.

Was he courageous in action? Did he overcome his fears by pursuing his task wholeheartedly? Did he overcome despair by focusing his attention on the satisfactions he found in performing this futile task? Did he share his courage or despair with his companions? Did he exhibit feelings of hatred? Or did he respect the feelings of his companions and show that respect in his actions?

In this image of his own feelings and the behavior they motivate, he also experiences himself at his utmost, because this is how he is, this is what he feels, and this is how he behaves when he is free to do his utmost.

While the performer is doing his utmost, he must also formulate a clearly defined conception of honorable human conduct. Perhaps he may value this as a conception of himself at his best, and he may value the sport experience because it permits him to see himself in this light. It is also possible, however, that he accepts the terms of this code only insofar as they permit him to enjoy the integrative experience, or perhaps only insofar as they permit him to do his utmost to make his own best possible score.

We must examine these possibilities more closely, because we cannot interpret the meanings men find in sport apart from them. Perhaps we can find some clues to the conflicts within these possibilities by returning to the story of the Greek warriors who developed this conception in the funeral games.

Like Sisyphus, these Greek warriors of three thousand years ago formulated their conception of the forces that controlled the universe in personal terms. They pictured their gods as supermen and superwomen and assigned to each of them absolute control over certain forces that structured the realities of the universe and the realities of their own existence within it.

On occasion, these gods could be kind and generous; but more often they were capricious, treacherous, cruel, self-seeking, and destructive. In life, as in the competition of the funeral games, each god seemed to have his own favorites, and each had his own reasons for wanting to punish one or more of the mortal men who were competing. Thus they facilitated the efforts of their favorites and interfered with the efforts of those who had incurred their wrath.

Usually, the Greek warriors felt no compunction about being equally capricious, treacherous, cruel, and destructive in their dealings with those who opposed their own self-seeking efforts. But when they undertook the task of formulating a conception of man at his utmost, they did not permit themselves to behave in these self-seeking ways.

Rather, every man agreed that he would not seek advantage for himself at the expense of other men and that he would not hamper any other man's efforts. In this sense, they were demanding much more of themselves than they expected of the capricious and treacherous gods who controlled the lives of men; that is, the moral code they defined transcended the natural behavior of the universe and imposed a new set of human values upon it.

But we must not make the mistake of seeing these rough warriors as Greek philosophers engaged in philosophical debate about human values, because they did not arrive at this conception of human honor and dignity by theorizing about it. They were practical men, concerned with practical matters. What each man really wanted was a fair chance to demonstrate his own competence in performing the symbolic actions of the funeral games; but in order to ensure his own fair chance he found he had to ensure an equal opportunity to all other competitors.

Thus, in their own self-seeking and practical ways, these rough warriors formulated a code of human ethics in the functional terms of human action. And, later, as they tried to act in the ways prescribed by this code, they also actualized all the human conflicts inherent in the idealistic belief that all men are entitled to the same opportunity to do their utmost to become whatever they are capable of being.

In the ethical codes of sport, we may find the patterns of many religious codes or we may find the patterns of democracy.

In this sense, we may see the sport arena as a functional laboratory for exploring the implications of those codes. But Homer did not suggest that the Greek warriors entered into sport for the purpose of exemplifying these ideals. Rather, each man accepted the terms of these ideals as the conditions which made it possible for him, personally, to do his utmost to demonstrate his own ability to perform his own chosen sport task. Nonetheless, let it be said to the credit of these warriors, and to the credit of sport, that they did, in fact, honor this idealistic code in action while they were engaged in sport competition. And so has every sport performer worthy of the name from that day to this.

Within the realistic terms of their own lives, however, the Greek warriors did not actually honor this idealistic code of ethical human behavior. Nonetheless, in the arguments that followed each sport event they interpreted each other's sport behavior in terms of a larger conception of their own honor as noblemen. Perhaps then we may assume that they really did believe that all noblemen would behave, or should behave, in this ethical fashion if the gods gave them a fair chance to function at their utmost. And perhaps we may find this interpretation in every performer's acceptance of the demand that he must allow every man to function at his utmost while he performs in the symbolic world of sport.

The experience of submitting himself to the rules that govern the symbolic world of sport provides each performer with access to many complex conceptions of himself at his utmost, and each of these conceptions offers many complex sources of meaning. But, paradoxically, the rules of sport prohibit him from thinking about those meanings while he is involved in the sport experience. These conceptions are formulated wholly within the terms of the performer's interest in one specific and well-defined task; and while he is performing that task, he must focus all his attention and all his energies upon it.

As he does his utmost to perform this specific task, he may

develop a conception of the quality of his own performance; the score denotes this qualitative conception in quantitative terms. If this score is relatively high, he may well value it as evidence of his own ability to perform that specific task, whatever it may be. But if it is low, he need not be unduly concerned about it because the task, as such, is utterly trivial and has no lasting effect on any material form. In this case, we may say that the performer seems to value the experience of making the score far more than he values the score as such. Perhaps he does, but we must also recognize that he finds those experiences meaningful within the terms of one very specific sport task. He may however find little meaning in similar sport forms, and he may find many sports virtually meaningless.

We now turn our attention to the specific patterns of a few representative sport forms to see what connotations we may find in them—always recognizing, of course, that each man's connotations are his own and that no two performers are obliged to find each other's meanings in any form.

The Greek warriors developed the prototype of the symbolic world of sport by devising the forms called javelin throwing, discus hurling, wrestling, foot racing, and chariot racing. As they stood "naked before their gods" in the sacred grove of Olympia, they found the performance of those forms meaningful, even as men in the twentieth century may find them meaningful in their modern version of the Olympic Games.

But human inventiveness was not exhausted by the creation of these classic sport forms. In every period of their history, men have invented new sport versions of the futile task of Sisyphus which seem to represent new ways of imposing their own conceptions of a possible set of SFRs upon the universe.

As we examine the patterns within the enduring Olympian sport forms, we may recognize that these events test the ability to overcome the inertia of a heavy organization of mass by sheer force of individual muscular power. Only in the chariot races were the competitors permitted to extend their own powers by using a horse-drawn vehicle, and even here the competitor's own muscular powers were severely tested by his attempts to control the horses as he urged them onward.

This characteristic pattern takes on more significance when we note that the warrior kings of early Greece, no less than the slaves who served them, entered into face-to-face combat with their opponents, armed only with their own personal power in moving the heavy weapons of war. And in the rare periods of peace, these same kings worked with the heavy materials of the universe in this same way, aided only by such simple mechanical devices as levers and wheels.

This was an age of "rugged individualism," in which each king ruled his own small domain by the power of his own personal might, competing with other warrior kings far more often than he cooperated with them in some mutual endeavor. In the end, they all succeeded in destroying each other, but we cannot retrace that long and brutal story here. Rather, we may comment that they did not develop any sport forms that required cooperation among a team of men. We may also note that the privileges of the symbolic world of sport were available only to these powerful men, each of whom traced his own ancestry to the gods. The lesser men who sought their protection could not enter the lists against them, and of course, their slaves were barred from competition, even though many of them were noblemen in their own right and had been reduced to slavery only because they had been on the losing side in realistic competitions of war.

In short, only freemen who could trace their ancestry to one of the Greek gods were eligible to display their powers in the early Olympian festivals, which honored Zeus, the father of all gods. And all the distinctions between "amateur" and "professional" can be traced to this early conception of a "nobleman" as a person who did his chosen work because he wanted to, and not because he had been forced to do it or was being paid for his efforts.

In time, however, the descendants of these noblemen did open the lists at Olympia to other freemen who were not able to claim direct descent from the gods. And in time, too, they recognized that a workman might pursue sport as a "professional" without sacrificing his personal honor. But, knowingly or unknowingly, they recognized that the injection of any thought of material rewards destroys the basic conceptions of sport, as such, and they assigned the professional athlete to a special category and denied him the right to compete in amateur terms.

The kings and noblemen of feudal Europe developed more advanced techniques for overcoming the inertia of the universe, and they introduced new actions into the symbolic world of sport. As they jousted with each other in colorful tournaments, each man demonstrated his own prowess and honor by showing what he could do with these new implements.

The peasants who labored in the fields did not participate in these tournaments. In time of war they served their noble protectors by pooling their strength in cooperative attempts to push heavy battering rams through the gates of the walls that protected the castle of the enemy, and in rare times of peace they survived as best they could by huddling together in their miserable villages.

Perhaps these cooperative experiences led them to discover that men who are individually inconsequential can sometimes achieve substantial purposes by working together. Perhaps not. But in either case, these hard-working peasants developed the prototype of all team sports.

These team forms began as crude rock-pushing contests in which the peasants reenacted their attempt to push a battering ram through the gates of the walls that surrounded the confines of the enemy. Today, this conception of the gate still survives in the symbolic goalposts which are common to all outdoor team sports.

These early rock-pushing contests were little more than mass mayhem, but gradually they were defined by established rules and well-recognized patterns of organization. Within this evolutionary process, the heavy rock was gradually reduced to the size and shape of a ball, and this small globe became the object of contest in many different team sports.

Much has been written about the ball as a symbolic representation of the earth. Perhaps the peasants who developed these new ball-using sports noticed this resemblance; more probably they were not consciously aware of it. But in either event it may be noted that the ball became an important object of contest in sport at about the time men discovered that their earth was indeed a sphere, or globe.

As feudal Europe was gradually reorganized into the more complex social patterns of the Renaissance, the old feudal lords were transformed into a new class called gentlemen. These gentlemen did not work with their hands; they did not maintain their social position by displays of muscular power. Rather, they prided themselves on their ability to deal with the world with wit and skillful use of strategic devices. These gentlemen exhibited little interest in the rough team sports in which men who were individually inconsequential used their muscular strength in cooperative endeavors. Rather, they developed new sport forms which symbolized their ways of performing a gentleman's tasks.

In these forms, exemplified by tennis and golf, each man performed alone, or perhaps with one partner, and his opponent or opponents were men of equal social rank. The rules for these sports prohibited any form of body contact between players, and there was little direct contact between any performer and the object of contest. Rather, a light ball was manipulated with a device or an implement which greatly extended the player's reach and force; the objective of the contest was formulated in terms of skill, dexterity, and strategy rather than in terms of muscular strength.

Did these gentlemen recognize the resemblance between their sport effort and their conception of themselves as gentlemen who manipulated the things of earth with ease, skill, and light implements? Probably not. But we may conjecture that they found satisfaction in these sports because they were consonant with their self-image.

Moving now toward our own time, we may note that the invention of new sport forms in which the ball is used as an object of contest ended in the nineteenth century, with the introduction of the American game of basketball in 1891 and volleyball in 1895. The new sport forms which have emerged during the twentieth century exhibit very different patterns of organization.

Today, men have extended their concern for the earthly globe to a vision of the farthest reaches of the universe, and their expectations of exploring the universe are based on their mastery over complex machines and electronic sources of power. Both of these conceptions are reflected in the new sport forms developed in recent years.

In scuba diving, for example, the diver utilizes the discoveries of modern science to equip himself for his descent into the depths of the sea. In sky diving, the diver utilizes the man-made power of mechanical flight to carry himself to the heights of the sky, from which he descends with great skill, using his parachute only in the final moments of the dive. In all forms of mechanized racing, men control the power of motorized vehicles on land, on sea, and in the air; and in such modern events as the destruction derby, they use these vehicles as implements in machine-to-machine combat.

This is not to suggest that the sportsman has transferred the effort or danger of sport to his machines. Rather, he has used the power of his man-made devices to extend the demands he imposes on himself. In each of these new forms, he knowingly exposes himself to great danger, and in each form he finds a way to surmount that danger as he explores the limits of his ability to deal with the inertia of mass-space-time in the larger dimensions of the universe.

As the men of every age and every culture have found new ways to deal with the forces of the universe, they have devised new sport forms to project these new images of what man can do and be at his utmost. In this sense, we may see the athlete as an explorer, drawn or driven by his own need to test the limits of human ability within the terms of these new conceptions of the task of Sisyphus. Or we may see these new sport forms as creative ventures into the still unknown and untried dimensions of human accomplishment and understanding.

But we need not limit this interpretation to the emergent sport forms which represent the emerging aspirations of men. Is not the javelin thrower who seeks to excel all previous records set by men equally creative? Is he not also using his human ingenuity to devise better techniques for overcoming the inertia of the massive forms of the universe? Is he not also seeking to extend the limits of human achievement?

Within this interpretation, we may see all would-be champions as creative people who extend the limits of human performance, even as the creative scientist or artist may extend the limits of human understanding. Drawn or driven by his own human need to impose his understanding of the SFRs of the universe upon its material forms, he may commit his life to the development of his ability to perform one specific feat, even as a scientist may commit his life to discovering the SFRs in one specific organization of materials.

In the intensity of his concentration on this one goal, he may seem oblivious to the social demands imposed by family, friends, and community. He may be, and often is, personally unpopular. But he may also count the world well lost if he succeeds in adding one split second or one millimeter to the records of human accomplishment.

Why does he choose to specialize in this particular feat? Probably for the same reasons that one scientist may devote his life to the SFRs of soap bubbles, and another may find the SFRs of plutonium more interesting.

Perhaps he chooses his particular sport form because it formulates his conception of himself as a man who performs certain kinds of work. This theory is supported by the evidence of history; it has also been supported by evidence found in several population studies of the sport interests of selected people who perform similar kinds of work. But we may also find many exceptions to the theory that the performer finds the meanings of his own work in his chosen sport.

Perhaps he chooses his particular sport form because his own physical being seems to be so admirably designed for the performance of this specific task. This theory is supported by many descriptions of the physical characteristics of the performers in selected sports. But, again, we may find many individual exceptions to this theory.

Perhaps he chooses his particular sport form because it formulates the basic patterns of his own personality structure. This theory is supported by evidence of certain relationships between the emotional patterns of sport and the patterns of the performer's own emotional organization. However, we must interpret this theory cautiously, because such relationships may be demonstrated in a variety of ways, each of which demands its own interpretation.

Perhaps he chooses his sport form because he was introduced to it at an early age, and as he became involved in the challenge it provided, he continued to pursue that challenge without need to examine his reasons for pursuing it. Or perhaps he chooses it for the same reason the mountain climber chooses to scale Mt. Everest—simply because it is there.

But whatever the influencing factors may be, we know that he undertakes the performance of this task for the most valid of all human reasons; he involves himself in the effort of performing this task because it interests him and because he finds that involvement meaningful in its own right.

Logically, we must not ask him to try to explain the meanings he finds in this involvement. He found them in a nonverbal form, and his understanding of them must always defy full verbal expression. Moreover, he found them in the connotations of the form, and in sport, as in dance, no man can attempt to denote connotations without destroying the image in which he finds them.

As we turn from the champion performer to the perpetual duffer, there is little need to modify our interpretation of the meanings he may find in sport. In the world of reality, the duffer's Mt. Everest may seem to be a very insignificant hill, but in the symbolic world of sport it demands his utmost effort and involves the utmost reaches of his being.

Potentially, any task that he pursues within the rules of sport might make these meanings available to him, but he usually chooses a sport that formulates his conception of man at his utmost in terms that reflect his own personal interest in his work, his physical being, or his own personality.

When he does find a task that formulates the image of his interests in particularly meaningful terms, he may well be endlessly fascinated with the process of pursuing that task, even though he knows that his scores will never add one cubit to the image of man's utmost ability to perform this trivial feat. Secure in the knowledge that the world will not be changed by his performance of this inconsequential task, he is free to pursue his own interest in it wholeheartedly, solely because he finds it interesting. In the process, he may also be re-created, integrated, and physiologically stimulated; but he has no need to justify his pursuit of a trivial task in terms of these concomitant effects. Rather, he may value the experience of pursuing a trivial task in the symbolic world of sport for what it is in its own right; he may value it because it creates a meaningful image of himself at his utmost.

But what about girls and women? Is sport also a symbolic formulation of "woman at her utmost"? In general, yes, but in the specific terms of some sports, no. In every age, these answers have been framed in terms of prevailing conceptions of what a female is and what kinds of work she may do within the social patterns of her time. In our own time, women are performing many kinds of work with dignity and honor. Equally, they are finding their own images of woman at her utmost in many parallel forms of sport. And in both work and sport, their choices reflect their own definitions of the feminine image which is currently acceptable within their own social milieu.* But within these cultural interpretations of roles appropriate for women, everything we have said about sport forms would seem to apply equally to both sexes.

Turning now to the spectators who watch other men perform in sport, we may again return to the Greek warriors, because they also developed the prototype of sport as a presentational form.

In time, the competitions that portrayed "the excellence of Patroclus" were transferred to the sacred grove of Olympia and presented in honor of Zeus, the father of all the gods. We do not know when the first presentation occurred, but the tradition of holding these festivals was firmly established by the year 776 B.C., and from that time onward, all Greek history was dated in terms of these Olympiads.

These formal presentations of man at his utmost attracted many spectators. Perhaps they were drawn to Olympia by their interest in the other competitions in which men demonstrated their ability in song, poetry, oratory, and other forms of human accomplishment. But undeniably they all sought entrance to the stadium and sat naked on the dry grass in the heat of the burning sun in order to pursue their interest in sport.

As these spectators watched each competitor project his own image of man at his utmost, they saw only the visible outlines of his performance. Perhaps they were interested in the patterns created by his movements as he attempted to over-

---

* I have developed the thesis of "Sport and the Feminine Image" in Connotations of Movement in Sport and Dance, William C. Brown Company, Publishers, Dubuque, Iowa, 1965.

come the inertia of his chosen organization of materials. Perhaps they marveled at the efficiency displayed by some performers and noted the clumsiness of others. But, in general, they were interested in what those movements accomplished. Or we may say that they were interested in the accomplishments denoted by the score.

Perhaps they recognized that the scores of all competitors who obeyed the rules of sport projected the image of "the excellence of Patroclus" with equal force, but they were not equally interested in the scores of all competitors. Rather, they singled out those competitors who came from their own city-state, gloried in their accomplishments, and claimed them as their own.

In the early Olympiads, the competitors who represented the various city-states were freemen who came from families that claimed the gods as their ancestors. They were amateurs in the strictest sense of the term; presumably the only prize they sought was a laurel wreath, which began to wither even as the judges placed it on the victor's head.

Historians have found many meanings in this symbolic wreath of victory. Some have suggested that even as the wreath withered, so must the victor's pride in his accomplishments. Others have found it to mean that the glory of sport is in the striving, rather than in the achieving. Both of these conceptions are represented in the idea that the victor cannot "rest on his laurels" after he has won them. Rather, he must renew his efforts to perform at his utmost within the realistic arena of life.

Perhaps the spectators also found these meanings in the victor's wreath, but they soon negated them by heaping many material rewards upon the victorious representatives of their communities. Sometimes they symbolized their civic pride in the accomplishments of these representatives by tearing down portions of the walls that surrounded the city to indicate that a city which could boast of such a citizen had no need for other protection against its enemies. And at times they rewarded their successful representatives by giving them free meals and lodgings for the rest of their lives, according them places of honor in the civil affairs of the community, and exempting them from military service.

In time the city-states found victory at Olympia so desirable that each city sought out the best athletes it could find and induced them to represent the community by making them honorary citizens and promising them substantial rewards for every victory. At first this was done surreptitiously, but eventually the practice became so common that professional athletes were openly admitted to competition at Olympia and elsewhere as legitimate representatives of any community that might hire their services.

About this time, the freemen who claimed to be descended from the gods seemed to lose interest in the Olympiads. Perhaps they could no longer find an image of their own interests in the efforts of men who openly sought material rewards for their performances in the symbolic world of sport. Or perhaps their lack of interest could be traced to the fact that many of them were no longer preoccupied with the kinds of tasks that involved overcoming the inertia of mass with their own muscular forces. In any event, the men who called themselves intellectuals found little interest in the performances of these professional athletes, and some of them wrote scathing denunciations of their efforts and their motivations.

In contrast, the artisans, farmers, and other men who worked for a living seemed to find a clearer image of their own interests in the performances of these city employees; they honored and rewarded athletes for enhancing the reputation of the workers' communities and paid them handsomely for their efforts. Also, workmen frequented the games in ever-increasing numbers and established new festivals which provided opportunities for all men to watch their champions in action.

Throughout the long years of history, the distinction between amateur and professional performers has been debated and redebated by the philosophers of sport. Today, few specta-tors seem to be interested in that distinction. In fact, intellectuals and workmen alike often prefer to watch professional perform-ers, if only because so many of the most distinguished per-formers now "turn pro." Also, they choose to watch only the best amateur performers at any level and show little interest in the efforts of millions of other boys, girls, men, and women who daily project their own images of man at his utmost in informal and intramural sport competitions.

This exclusive interest in watching only the best performers suggests that most spectators are seeking the meanings we found in the champion's conception of the utmost that man can accomplish, rather than those we found in the duffer's more modest conception of himself at his utmost. In this sense, we might say that the performances of the champions provide the spectators with symbolic evidence of the farthest reaches of man's ability to accomplish his human purposes.

Many philosophers have interpreted the meaning of the Olympian competitions in these terms, and perhaps we may assume that the gods who looked down from Mt. Olympus found this meaning in the symbolic evidence of man's accom-plishments. But the mortal spectators who sat on the dry grass of earth did not seem to be interested in this exalted conception. Rather, each spectator seemed to be most interested in the image of himself, as he found it in some performer who seemed to represent his personal interests in some way.

While the performance was in progress, his own feelings seemed to reflect the feelings of the performer he had chosen as his personal representative in the symbolic world of sport. The spectator did everything he could to urge that performer to do his utmost. When his representative did well, his own spirits rose; and when his alter ego tripped or fell or failed in any way, he shared his feelings of dejection and despair. He also gloried in his representative's courage, his determination, and his resolute efforts to do his utmost in the face of defeat.

Perhaps he recognized the excellence of other performers, and perhaps he applauded that excellence. But although he might congratulate any victor on his accomplishments, he rejoiced wholeheartedly only when the symbolic wreath was placed on the head of his own personal representative.

Some philosophers have been appalled by the self-interest of these spectators, claiming that it tarnishes the ideals of Olympian competition. In terms of the larger meanings they find in this symbolic image of man at his utmost, they argue that every performer is equally representative of the whole human race, and every spectator should glory equally in the accomplishments of all champions, whoever they may be.

But here we must defend the spectator's selfish interest in the accomplishments of his personal representative by identifying it as the basis of his ability to understand the meanings of sport as a symbolic form. As we traced the sources of those meanings, we found them in the performer's emotional involvement in his own efforts to produce a symbolic score, and we recognized that those meaningful emotions were generated only if the performer played to win. Or we may say that the performer would find little interest in the terms of any sport contest if he had no personal interest in doing his utmost to win the game.

The spectator, too, must experience the feelings of playing to win in order to experience the important meanings generated by any sport competition. Like the performer, he must care very much about his personal stake in the contest, because without this self-interest the terms of sport competition are virtually meaningless. In this sense, we may say that the spectator activates the most basic meanings of sport by championing the interests of one performer and team and valuing them above the interests of all other performers.

Perhaps he recognizes the performer, or team, as his personal emissary because he represents his own community, educational institution, or some other socially organized group.

Perhaps he merely identifies a team as his own, even though he has no connection with it other than emotional attachment. Or perhaps, if he is watching a contest between two unknown teams, he may choose his side in terms of some unknown factor, which is probably his own tendency to identify himself as a "loser" or a "winner." Thus, he may glory in the goals made by a sandlot team of "jaguars" and suffer every time the "panthers" make a basket, even though he knows nothing about the members of either team and may not even know their language.

Within the limits of his capacity for sharing the feelings of other men, the spectator may find the performer's meanings in any sport form. Perhaps he chooses one form rather than another because it symbolizes his conception of himself at work. Perhaps he chooses one particular version of the task of Sisyphus simply because it is there or because he finds it interesting. Or perhaps he chooses a sport form that projects the image of his own emotional patterns and permits him to actualize those emotions that are most meaningful to him.

But we must not ask the spectator to explain the meanings he finds in watching the performances of the champions. In all probability he cannot explain those meanings to himself. But this does not matter. He has made those meanings his own by experiencing them within the innermost reaches of his own feelings, and in experiencing them, he has found a meaningful image of himself at his utmost.

CHAPTER 7

EXERCISE FORMS

... the act of finding
What will suffice.

An exercise form is an organization of movements.

Theoretically, the performance of these movements will have certain desirable effects on the being of the performer, and the person performs those movements for the purpose of producing those effects.

The conception of such an organization of movements is clearly defined in the description of the exercise; the conception of its probable effects is usually identified in general terms.

The performance of the exercise denotes this conception of an organization of movements, but it does not necessarily denote the conception of the desired effects.

Other conceptions may be connoted by the SFRs of the performance or by any recognizable set of SFRs within it.

The man-made movement forms called exercise have a good name but a bad reputation. Theoretically, they are designed to serve the purposes of self-improvement. If they are appropriately selected and consistently performed, they usually do have this desirable effect. But alas, although many people extol the self-improving virtues of exercise, they find its realities boring, demanding, and tiresome; and even while they recognize their own need for its benefits, they forego improvement in order to avoid its tiresome demands.

In all fairness to exercise, however, we must also recognize that many people do embrace its demands wholeheartedly and pursue its beneficial effects through all the years of their lives. Perhaps these people are made of sterner stuff than the lesser mortals who reject such opportunities for self-improvement, or perhaps it is only that they have a better understanding of the potentialities of exercise as a man-made movement form. In either case, their behavior provides us with clean-cut evidence of some of the meanings men may find in exercise, and so we shall keep their example before us as we begin our analysis of the characteristics of all exercise forms.

An exercise is an organization of movements. These movements were devised for the purpose of producing certain effects on the being of the performer. These effects may be described in anatomical, physiological, or psychological terms; but here we may include all these terms in the general conception of improving the functional capacity of the person in some way.

These movements may be very simple. An exercise, for example, may consist in nothing more than raising the arms and lowering them. These movements may also be very complex, consisting in a series of very complicated actions which require precise use of every segment of the body. These actions may be easy to perform, or they may be exceedingly difficult. They may be interesting to the performer, or they may be wholly devoid of interest. But whatever the characteristics of these movements may be, the performer executes them because he believes the exercise will be good for him in some way. Or we may say that the performer is interested in the effects those movements have on his being rather than in the movements, as such.

In order to produce those effects, the performer must execute the prescribed movements precisely, he must repeat them again and again, and he must continue doing this day after day in precisely the same manner. While he is performing the exercise, he must keep his attention focused on the prescribed movements, and he must focus all the energies of his being on the effort to perform those movements precisely and vigorously.

At the time of these many repetitions, his interest may be sustained by the hope of future benefits, but he does not experience those benefits during the performance. Rather, he experiences the immediate effects of these movements; paradoxically, these effects are usually quite opposite to the long-term benefits they may ultimately produce.

If the exerciser hopes to increase the functional strength of certain muscles, for example, he must perform an exercise that will fatigue those muscles; during the exercise he experiences this fatigue, rather than the increase in strength which may ultimately result from it.

If he is interested in improving the functional efficiency of his heart and circulatory system, he must perform an exercise that will leave him breathless and panting; during the exercise he will experience the rapid pounding of his heart, rather than the more efficient cardiovascular functioning that may eventually result from this experience.

If he seeks to improve his ability to adapt to stress, he must stress every physiological system to its utmost during the exercise, and he will experience this maximal response to stress, rather than the more effective adaptational responses he hopes for.

If he wishes to improve the functional capacity of his shoulder joint so that he can move his arm more freely, he must perform an exercise that actually stretches the ligaments and fascia in that area; during the exercise he will experience the feeling of being stretched to his utmost limits, rather than the feeling of moving freely and without restriction.

If he hopes to improve his capacity for using his muscles more effectively, he may perform an exercise that decreases the tension in all his muscle fibers and leaves him utterly limp, and during the exercise he will experience that limpness, rather than the greater functional efficiency that may result from it.

And if his purpose is to decrease his body weight, he must perform an exercise which actually consumes many calories of energy, but he will experience this caloric consumption as breathlessness or fatigue, rather than as the process of "burning up fat."

The exerciser may find the immediate effects of his own movements interesting in their own right, but unless he has some understanding of the principles of human physiology, he may have difficulty in recognizing the connection between these effects and the ultimate "good" he hopes to derive from the exercise. And here we must recognize that this hope may be betrayed by the lack of such understanding.

Only an exercise that is wholly appropriate to the needs, abilities, and aspirations of the performer can accomplish this ultimate good. An exercise that is badly chosen may have no lasting effect on the being of the performer or may damage his functional capacity rather than improve it.

If the performer attempts to execute an exercise that is beyond his strength, for example, he may bring other segments of his body into play in an awkward attempt to exert greater force; in his awkwardness he may damage tendons, ligaments, and fascial tissues to such an extent that he will be stiff and sore for a long time. Or if he pushes his own physiological systems beyond the limits of their ability to adjust to the functional needs of his body, he may exhaust himself to such a degree that he cannot immediately recover from the effects of fatigue, and he may be tired and inefficient for a long time after the exercise is completed.

Fortunately, cardiologists have assured every exerciser that a normal heart will not be ultimately damaged by the demands of exercise, but if the exerciser's heart is already compensating for some minor functional deficiency, it may decompensate under excessive demands, and the deficiency may be exaggerated by this experience.

In stretching the ligaments and fascia around his shoulder joint, the exerciser may actually tear them, and as a consequence of these minute tears, any attempt to move his arm may be painful. And of course, there is always the possibility that the weight-reducing exercise may increase his hunger to such an extent that he will eventually take in far more calories than he has consumed during the exercise.

We must recognize, too, that the exerciser who knows little about the SFRs of his own internal functioning is often overly optimistic about the dimensions of the ultimate good he may derive from any exercise. In his ignorance of these matters, he may expect to be transformed into a superman by the effects of a few simple movements. But he must experience this transformation in terms of some rather subtle changes in his conception of himself as a functional human being, and often he may be scarcely aware of these modest changes in his own functional capacity.

As we begin our search for the meanings the performer may find within the complexities of these experiences, we must remind ourselves again that each man's connotations are his own. We may also need to remind ourselves of this again and again as we search our own experiences for clues to these possible connotations, because here, too, we shall find that every image of exercise has two opposing faces.

Beginning with our conception of the exerciser's purpose, we may find in it a gratifying image of self-improvement, but hidden within this idea is the recognition that the person stands in need of such improvement because he is not as "good" as he might be, could be, or should be. Thus, he may embrace the idea of exercise because it promises him a gratifying reward, but he may be resistant to that idea because it reflects an unfavorable image of himself as a deficient or inadequate human being.

These conceptions of personal adequacy or inadequacy may be reinforced by his experiences with the exercise, and equally they may be negated or dispelled by those experiences. If he is able to perform the "improving" patterns of movement easily and without distress, he may experience himself as being strong, flexible, agile, inexhaustible, and generally effective; and he may be gratified by this image of himself. Conversely, if he has difficulty in executing the movement patterns, he may experience himself as being weak, clumsy, and generally ineffective; and his sense of inadequacy as a human being may be reinforced by these distressing images.

As he interprets the movement patterns in terms of his conception of himself, his feelings of personal adequacy or inadequacy may be similarly enhanced or diminished. For example, if he recognizes the conception of gracefulness in certain movements, he may either welcome, resist, or be indifferent to the opportunity to perform those patterns; and as he performs them, either gracefully or dis-gracefully, he may find this self-knowledge either gratifying, uninteresting, or depressing.

Similarly, he may welcome or resist a particular exercise because of the implications he finds in the positions, postures, or actions it requires. Some performers resist lying face downward on the floor, perhaps because they find in this position the implications of submission or defeat or because they do not like to have their visual awareness limited to the dimensions of the floor or the exercise mat or because they find the odors of the floor or mat offensive. Other performers may welcome this position, perhaps because it permits them to hide their faces or their bodies from other performers. Conversely, some performers resist lying on their backs with arms and legs stretched out, perhaps because they feel exposed in all their personal inadequacy, but others seem to welcome this personal exposure.

Some performers respond favorably to the implications they find in the action of reaching upward or in "stretching up tall" or in twisting and turning; others enjoy the feeling of limpness and nonaction they find in a "relaxation exercise." Other performers may resist the implications of these actions and sensations without understanding why they feel personally diminished by them.

A performer may see the action of running in place as an essay in futility, and this interpretation may reinforce his image of himself as a person who never seems to "get anywhere." Another may interpret the action pattern of sit-ups as an image of his ability to use his personal forces effectively under difficult circumstances. Perhaps some find an image of their own sexual prowess in their ability to perform push-ups. Others may find an image of their own neatness, precision, and careful workmanship in the carefully precise movements of a coordination routine. And perhaps others find an image of themselves as dancers in the complicated footwork of such exercises. And perhaps, perhaps, perhaps . . . because the connotations each performer may find in the process of using his own body in highly structured ways are beyond our imagining.

As the performer does use his body in these highly structured ways, his movements serve to intensify the functioning of various physiological processes. Perhaps his heart is stimulated to beat more rapidly; perhaps he contracts his muscles more forcibly; perhaps he stretches his fascia beyond their resting length; perhaps he increases or decreases the tonus of his muscles. In this sense, the exercise offers him an opportunity to experience himself at his utmost in certain dimensions of his being; and he may find many connotations in the conceptions of his own breathlessness, his own pounding heart, his own vertigo, his own muscle contractions, his own range of movement around every articulating joint, and the increase or decrease of his own muscle tonus.

As he experiences these sensory images of himself at his utmost, he also experiences his own feelings about himself as he interprets these sensations in personal terms. And in these interpretations he also finds an image of himself and an image of his own feelings about himself as a functional human being. In this sense, we may say that he actualizes his own feelings about himself within the exercise experience, but we must also recognize that he has time to rationalize those feelings and find acceptable interpretations of them during the many repetitions of the exercise.

Turning now to the long-term effects of exercise, we may recognize that these, too, must be evaluated in terms of the connotations the performer finds in them. Some men find the conception of being stronger intensely meaningful in terms of their self-image, others may not care one way or the other about this conception of their own strength, and still others may find the image of great muscular strength distasteful.

Similarly the conceptions of physiological endurance, adaptation to stress, freedom to move, relaxation, and body weight may seem desirable, uninteresting, or undesirable in terms of our own images of ourselves as adequate human beings. Perhaps some of these conceptions reflect a masculine image, others, an image of femininity, and we may find them pleasing or displeasing in terms of our own sexuality. Perhaps they reflect an image of a person who does certain kinds of work, and this image may reinforce or run counter to our own images of ourselves as competent workers who pursue the task of Sisyphus in our own chosen way. Or perhaps they reflect an image of a personality structure which reinforces or runs counter to our own emotional organization.

From the complexities of the many contradictory meanings that may be found in the experience of exercising, we can readily understand why exercise has a good name but a bad reputation. In general, however, we may say that this experience provides the exerciser with a meaningful image of himself at his utmost. If he finds that image gratifying, he may pursue the exercise wholeheartedly and be benefited by it; if he finds that image distressing, he may well find it virtually impossible to sustain his interest in it throughout all the repetitions that might produce those benefits. And so, many people who recognize their need for systematic exercise fail to satisfy that need, and many others find much satisfaction and enjoyment in doing what they know "is good for them."

On occasion, an exercise may be used as the basis of competition between two or more performers, perhaps informally or perhaps in terms of the conception of *free exercise* as it is used within the province of gymnastics. In such use, the exercise takes on all the properties of any sport form and may be interpreted in those terms as an image of man at his utmost, or perhaps in terms of the champion's image of the utmost ability of man.

On occasion, too, an exercise routine may be used as a presentational form and performed before an audience, with emphasis on the interests of the audience rather than the interests of the performers. In such use, the exercise routine takes on the properties of a dance form and must be interpreted as an organization of movement patterns, evoking whatever connotations the audience may find in them.

Regarding such competitions and presentations, the performer may forego the conception of the ultimate "good" he may derive from the exercise in favor of the meanings he finds in the immediate performance. And thus he may intensify his own awareness of any of the exceedingly complex meanings that may be found in exercise.

CHAPTER 8

"LEARNING TO MOVE—
MOVING TO LEARN"

A moving part of motion . . .
a change part of change,
. . . a discovery
Part of a discovery . . .
Too much like thinking
to be less than thought.

An educational form is an organization of experiences.

Theoretically, involvement in these experiences will induce the learning of certain conceptions or concepts.

These concepts are identified in the curriculum or program of studies adopted by the educational institution; usually, this curriculum also indicates how the learning of these concepts is to be evaluated.

The performance of these experiences denotes the learner's conception of the experiences; it does not denote what he learns from his involvement in them.

Evidence of this learning may be connoted by conceptions of his behavior during and after his involvement in the experiences; it may also be connoted by evidence of his ability to use certain symbols or symbolic forms in appropriate ways.

Other conceptions may be connoted by the SFRs of his involvement in these experiences and the SFRs of his subsequent behavior or by any recognizable set of SFRs within them.

Within the terms of this definition, education may be described as a process that serves to activate meaningful learning, or as a process that activates meanings.

The list of experiences that answer to the name of education in any area of human understanding is endless, and new experiences and new areas will be added to the list tomorrow and tomorrow and tomorrow, as long as man endures. Some of these experiences are so simple that a preschool-age child can involve himself in them, understand the conceptions they represent, and find much meaning in them. Others are so very complex that only a postdoctoral research worker in that area can deal with them in meaningful terms. Some require the use of material forms, and any material known to man may be used educationally. Others require only an understanding of certain concepts or constructs, and again there is no limit to the ideas that may be examined in the name of education. Some experiences demand that the learner move about; others require only quiet contemplation, or perhaps very small movements of the eyes or fingers, or perhaps only the ability to read or write or push a computerized device. But whatever characteristics they may have, all were devised in the same way and all may serve to activate the processes of human learning.

In general, the process of devising such meaningful experiences involves the knowledge and understanding of two kinds of experts, who may be called specialists and educators.

The specialists, who are knowledgeable about the concepts of some particular area of study, sort out the important conceptual constructs in their own field. Then they try to arrange them in an orderly sequence, beginning with the most general and ending with the most detailed or most complicated.

The educators, who are particularly knowledgeable about

the SFRs of the processes of human learning and about the needs, interests, and abilities of children and adults at various times in their lives, then attempt to devise experiences in which the conceptual constructs of the specialists are represented. They will also devise ways of involving the learners in these experiences by considering how the SFRs within them may be made most evident; they will consider how the learning that may accrue to these experiences is manifested and how it may be evaluated by the teacher.

The process of actually involving the potential learners in these experiences is initiated by a third kind of expert, called a teacher. This expert must have some understanding of the conceptual constructs identified by the specialists and much understanding of the complex processes of human learning and the complex needs, interests, and abilities of the learner. He must also be ingenious in devising methods for making the SFRs of the experience evident to the learner in ways that will engage his interest.

But the teacher cannot tell the learner how to learn or what to learn or what that learning means. Or we may say that every learner must do his own learning and find his own meanings, even as his unschooled ancestors did.

Moving about within the confines of the experience, the learner will perceive many forms and formulate many conceptions of the SFRs within them. He will think about those conceptions and try to relate them to his own comprehensive conception of reality and his conception of himself as a functional organization of the stuff of reality. He will hypothesize about the possibility of imposing new SFRs on the materials of the universe, and he will discover some measure of his ability to create new forms of his own devising. From these complex experiences, he will acquire certain skills and develop the habit of behaving in certain ways. And as he experiences feelings about himself and his discoveries, he will find his own meanings in what he has learned.

The teacher cannot explain these meanings to him; neither can he ask the learner to explain his own meanings. As we have recognized many times during the course of our search for the sources of meaning in dance, sport, and exercise, each man's connotations are his own, and he must find his own meanings in his own feelings about them. Or we may say that neither the teacher nor the learner can perform the paradoxical task of trying to denote connotations.

Thus, we must recognize that the learner may not find the teacher's meanings in his own understanding of the experience; perhaps this is fortunate for the advancement of human understanding, or perhaps not. In positive terms, however, the teacher recognizes that new knowledge is born of new insights into the meaning of old concepts, and so he will do everything he can to encourage the learners to develop the sources of their own human creativity.

The educational experiences that activate the meanings of movement are commonly assigned to the curriculum of physical education or to some extension of it within the school program.

In general, the specialists who identify the conceptual outlines of these experiences are knowledgeable about many aspects of movement and have studied it from many different points of view. Similarly, the educators who devise the experiences and the teachers who seek to involve the learners in them must have particular knowledge of the processes involved in learning to move and moving to learn.

As we tried to trace the sources of meaning in dance, sport, and exercise, we did not ask how the performer learned to move in these ways. Now, in view of our interest in the objectives of education, we must ask this question directly, even as we must admit that there is still much to learn about the internal dynamics of human learning.

At birth, all living creatures, both animal and human, seem to learn to move in much the same way. The representatives of each species exhibit certain characteristic coordinations which seem to be built into their biological structures, and these coordinations can be elicited by direct stimulation of the motor cortex during unconsciousness, not only at birth, but at any time during the life span. At birth, however, these characteristic coordinations may also be elicited by any strong stimulus, such as a bright light, loud noise, pressure, or withdrawal of support. One stimulus seems to serve as well as another, because the sensory system is not yet sufficiently developed to enable the infant to discriminate among the various kinds of sensations. Rather, the SFRs of these sensory images are blurred together in a vague, pervasive sense of "being alive," which is some-times described by the term "synesthesia."

Initially, the coordinations elicited by any sensation that is strong enough to disturb this synesthetic pattern are rather vaguely defined. These movements have an explosive or con-vulsive quality, and the infant's body oscillates in tremors of small amplitude—as if it were scanning itself for clues to the location of this disturbing sensation. Then, as each tremorous movement serves to modify the sensation in some way, the infant seems to sort out the effective or rewarding components within this sensorimotor interaction, and gradually, the move-ments become better organized and the tremors subside.

This seems to be what happens when a young bird is pushed or falls out of its nest. The feeling of falling elicits the built-in motor cortex patterns within the context of the scanning-type tremors and oscillations. At first, the bird seems to be thrashing around in the air as if it were trying to do something without quite knowing what. Then, movement by movement and sensation by sensation it seems to discover which ways of flapping its wings produce the rewarding feeling of being supported in air. In a few seconds, it has learned how to fly, and from then on it can begin to refine this skill and develop variations by this same trial-error-discovery process.

We may also trace the outlines of this process in the human

infant's performance as he develops the necessary skill of sucking. Or we may see it illustrated in the sink-or-swim method of learning to stay afloat in deep water. In general, it seems likely that, left to their own devices in their natural habitat, all animals develop their own built-in movement patterns and skills in this way.

Animal trainers and psychologists have used a more sophisticated version of this process to train lions in the skill of jumping through a hoop or to develop the skill of maze running in animals. Alas, we must also admit that some educators have also used this process to induce children to acquire specific skills, and perhaps some still do.

In these experiments, the skill to be learned is known to the trainer but not to the subject, and the trainer facilitates the discovery of the desired coordinations with externally applied forms of reward or punishment. Under these conditions, it has been shown that both animals and children can acquire a great variety of skills—but a number of carefully designed experiments have shown that animals and children do not learn these skills in quite the same way.

Given a relatively simple maze-learning problem, like a series of right and left turns, both dogs and children can learn to turn RLRL in a relatively small number of trials. But the children will learn the movement sequence more quickly, and they will remember it much longer.

If the maze pattern is more complicated, however, say RRLLRRLL, even the most intelligent dogs cannot quite master it, and they cannot retain their partial comprehension of the task. In contrast, any reasonably alert three-year-old child can learn such a sequence in a few trials and will remember it more or less indefinitely without need for repeated practice.

Obviously, then, the children are doing something the dogs cannot do. Rather than learning the pattern by rote, they seem to be dealing with some conception of the pattern, as a whole.

As soon as they grasp the idea of this pattern, they can move in accordance with it, even though they do not yet know the idea of right from the idea of left.

Other experiments have shown that human subjects do not necessarily deal with the experimenter's idea in the same way that he does. Rather, they act in terms of what the idea means to them, interpreting it within their own feelings about themselves and the realities of their existence, as they comprehend them. Thus, one subject may feel threatened by the idea of such actions, and another may welcome the opportunity to perform them; and these meanings will be "read into" the idea and evidenced in the performance of the actions. Accordingly, experimenters who use human subjects often have difficulty in interpreting their derived data in wholly objective terms.

The implications of man's ability to derive meaningful conceptions from such experiments may be illustrated by the familiar story of the ape who learned how to reach a banana that was suspended outside his cage. The ape eventually discovered that he could poke the experimenter's stick through the bars of the cage and bring down the banana; having done this once, he was able to do it again and again. We might say that he had learned the skill of reach extending.

But the ape could not apply this hard-won knowledge to other situations. When the stick was removed from the cage and a green banana put in its place, he did not recognize that the green banana had certain SFRs which resembled those of a reach-extending stick. Rather, he recognized it as a banana that was not fit to eat, pushed it aside as an object of no interest, and shook the bars of the cage that prevented him from reaching the yellow banana hanging just beyond arm's length.

In the same situation, an intelligent human being might waste a few minutes on the futile behavior of shaking the bars of his cage, but then he would start looking around for another object that exhibited the SFRs of a reach extender. If the green banana proved to be too short, he might then begin to experiment with ways of making his arm reach farther, perhaps call-ing on some of the ideas he had learned in his physical educa-tion classes. Yes, if he turned his side toward the bars, shifted his weight toward that foot, maneuvered his shoulder joint a bit, and relaxed the opposing muscles to permit maximum extension of elbow, wrist, and finger joints, he could reach a little farther; and he could use the green banana to extend his reach to where the edible banana was hanging.

In short, he could think about the SFRs within the situa-tion, hypothesize about how he might modify those SFRs in some way, and test his hypothesis by actually moving to impose a new set of SFRs on himself and the material forms available to him. If his idea worked, he would get the edible banana, but he would have much more than that. He would have a well-tested functional idea of the skill of reach extending which he could use again and again in many other situations.

We might also examine this difference by recalling our own experiences in trying to teach dogs and children new tricks. In teaching a tip-up or headstand, for example, we might begin by tipping both subjects upside down and pushing or pulling them into the balancing alignment, using our usual humane forms of reward and punishment to reinforce discovery and learning. In time, if we are patient, the dog will learn the trick, and he will be able to reproduce this alignment on signal. Perhaps the child will also learn the trick, or perhaps he will not, but in either case he will not approach the learning process in the same way.

If he becomes interested in doing a tip-up, there will come a moment when he will recognize some of the important SFRs within the trick, and every good teacher knows when this hap-pens. After that, pushing and pulling will only annoy him, be-cause he is ready to take over his own self-directed experimen-tation. Then the teacher can help most by giving verbal cues or light tactile cues which will help him clarify and amplify his understanding of this conception—supplemented, of course, by some judicious "spotting" to support him when a trial leads to error.

But if a child does not want to do a tip-up, no amount of humane pushing and pulling can force him to learn the skill. Or we may say that his experimental efforts will be guided by the meaning he finds in his feelings about this conception, rather than in the SFRs of the conception as such. If the idea is distasteful to him, or if he feels threatened by it in some way, he will not organize all the energies of his being into an attempt to perform that idea; in general, he will refuse to do this even if his teacher tries to force him.

The teacher may also help the learner find a clearer conception of the functional SFRs of the skill by demonstrating it, by describing it, by pointing out how it is like other more familiar actions, or by identifying other analogous SFRs in certain parts of the dynamic pattern. He may ask the learner to break down the pattern and study each of its parts separately before he tries to put all the parts together in a dynamic whole. And he may provide the learner with many opportunities to use his emerging skill within the larger context of many man-made movement forms that are meaningful in their own right.

He may also further the learner's understanding by describing some of the SFRs within the anatomical organization of his body and by explaining the SFRs of some of the physiological interactions the learner experiences as he moves. He may help the learner relate the SFRs of the skill to other circumstances of his life and suggest how it might be used to increase his functional capacity for work, or perhaps improve his appearance as well as his functional effectiveness.

Also, he may encourage the learner to explore the SFRs of his own ability to move by suggesting certain possibilities to him and asking him to experiment with these ideas in his own way. Or he may set certain problems for the learner and ask him to solve them experimentally. And at times he will ask the learner to devise new games, dances, and exercises and perhaps ask his fellow learners to perform them.

In short, there is no limit to the methods a teacher may use in his attempt to make the SFRs of a certain movement more evident to the learner. But no matter how ingenious the teacher may be, the student must ultimately do his own learning and find his own meanings in what he learns.

Accordingly, in the initial stages of each new learning experience, he will exhibit the movement patterns we observed as we watched a young bird learning to fly. If we watch him closely, we will see that his body is oscillating in tremors of small amplitude, as if he were scanning himself for clues to the SFRs of his own sensorimotor interactions. Or we may note that we all tremble in this way in moments of panic, when we do not know what to do or how to do it. Then movement by movement and sensation by sensation the learner seems to discover how to induce the muscle contractions that will produce the effective pattern of action, and gradually he learns how to coordinate his own movements in skillful ways.

In this sense, we may say that he learns to move by moving to learn, because he cannot learn to coordinate his own movements in any other way. But we must also add that he learns much more than skill in his physical education classes.

The list of conceptions, ideas, and concepts he may formulate within these complex movement experiences is endless. Perhaps we can suggest the scope of this list by recognizing that the learner may deal with these conceptions within any of the three modes of interpretation.

Like Sci, the scientist, he may be interested in the properties of *being*, and so he may ask: What is the nature of the material elements I recognize in this form? How are these elements organized? How do they function in relation to each other and in relation to other elements of reality?

Like Ven, the practical inventor, he may be interested in the *denotational* properties of these forms, and so he may ask: What idea is denoted by the recognizable SFRs of this form? How does this fully organized form function within the operational organization of the universe?

Like Pat, the artist, he may be interested in the *connotational* properties of these forms, and so he may ask: What conceptions, feelings, and emotions are connoted by the SFRs of the patterns that I recognize within these forms?

And like Fil, the philosopher, he must always ask: What meaning do I find in my own feelings about myself and my conception of reality as I consider the properties of being, denotation, and connotation in all symbolic forms?

Perhaps he will find gratifying or distasteful meanings in the symbolic processes of exercise, or he may find no meaning in these self-improving movements. Perhaps he will find Ath's meanings in the symbolic processes of sport; perhaps not. Perhaps, like Kor and Dan, he will find many important meanings in the symbolic processes of dance, or he may find them virtually meaningless. And perhaps he will find Ug's meanings in the processes of movement as he applies them to the requirements of his own life tasks, or he may not notice his own movements. Or he may find no meaning at all in the processes of physical education and consider its experiences absurd.

As Socrates thought about these things many centuries ago, he recognized that men must move in order to understand themselves. Only by moving their own bodies with and against the forces of the universe could the prisoners of the cave discover the objective forms of reality; only by moving could they discover the realities of their own lives as human beings.

Thus the cave men moved about, perceiving many forms of reality, speculating about the SFRs within them, developing hypotheses about how reality was organized and hypotheses about how they might reorganize the forms of reality to their own advantage. And as they tested those hypotheses by moving with, and against, the forces of the universe, they created their own human culture and found their own sources of meaning within it.

> . . . and so must every man move
> and so must every man find meaning . . .

APPENDIX FOR EDUCATORS

The fluctuations of certainty, the change
Of degrees of perception in the scholar's dark.

These pages are addressed to educators who may be interested in knowing how I have used the ideas of *Movement and Meaning* in my own teaching.

In general, I have used these materials in courses designed for graduate and undergraduate students in physical education, and I shall describe my teaching techniques in those terms. However, my colleagues have also used many of the experiences listed below at all instructional levels and in a wide variety of courses.

Most of the concepts developed in *Movement and Meaning* will be more meaningful to students if they develop them within the terms of their personal experiences. Accordingly, my students learn with Ug, Sci, Ven, Pat, Fil, Kor, Dan, and Ath by doing what they did. Usually I keep these learning experiences synchronized with the chapters of the book, but I may also anticipate concepts by asking students to work on an idea we have not yet discussed. This gives them a better opportunity to make their own discoveries, and it gives them more insight into the terms of these concepts when we do examine them in class.

In a graduate seminar centered on the ideas of *Movement and Meaning*, I usually use all the experiences listed below. In an undergraduate class for physical education or elementary education majors, where time may be more limited, I would give priority to those marked with an asterisk. In other courses, and at other levels, my colleagues have sometimes proceeded directly to some of the double-starred experiences without preliminary explanation; at other times they have used various other combinations which are appropriate to the immediate interests of the learners.

1.   List ten words or phrases that denote some conception of the SFRs you can recognize in a chalk stick, e.g., white, mark maker, round. Identify similar sets of SFRs in other forms. How is a chalk stick like a finger? A concrete wall? A baseball bat?

2.   Think about a container that might serve some specialized purpose, e.g., protecting food from flies. Using aluminum foil, construct a model of a bowl that might serve this purpose.

3.   Think about the SFRs you recognize in some particular piece of sport equipment, e.g., tennis racket. Using aluminum foil, construct a model of such a piece of equipment. Show your model to someone and explain to him how its structure is related to the functions you expect the equipment to perform.

4.   Think about some persistent human problem; e.g., when making soup, what does the cook do with the stirring spoon between stirrings? Or, how can a person open a container without need for supplementary equipment? Hypothesize about the possibility of devising a man-made form that would solve this problem. Test your hypothesis by constructing a model of such a form out of suitable or substitute materials. Bring your model to class and let the other students hypothesize about its possible functions. Then explain your idea, your form, and the relevant SFRs.

*5. Think about some persistent problem in dealing with the equipment needed in a physical education class; e.g., how can arrows be segregated according to length, weight, and markings and transported to the archery range by one person? Hypothesize, test, and explain as above.

*6. Apply this same process of thinking, hypothesizing, testing, and explaining to some problem in coordination; e.g., how can I rise from a lying position to a standing position without using my hands and arms? Or, how can I carry a glass of water on my head?

7. Think about your conception of the term *house*. Sketch the basic outlines of "what a house is" in the fewest possible pencil strokes or chalk marks. Compare your sketch with those made by other students and discuss the SFRs denoted by all sketches.

8. Think about your conception of the term *home*. Convert your sketch of the SFRs of a house into a representation of "what makes a house a home." Compare and discuss as before.

**9. Think about a game of tennis. Try to visualize some of the patterns and designs you can recognize within the SFRs of the game, e.g., court markings, path of ball, path of players. Sketch some of these patterns. Try to identify similar patterns in other forms and experiences, e.g., a screen, a fence, a wall, the trajectory of a bullet, the flight of a bird. Explain some of these resemblances.

**10. Think about a familiar dance. Visualize, sketch, and describe some of its patterns and designs.

11. Sketch a series of doodles. Using only straight lines, make the first sketch symmetrical, the second, asymmetrical.

Using only curved lines, sketch other symmetrical and asymmetrical designs. Study your designs and observe your own reactions to them. Which do you find most pleasing? Which are least interesting to you? Compare designs and reactions with those of other students.

12. Select your most interesting design and study its SFRs. Do they suggest the SFRs of any other familiar forms or experiences? Discuss these resemblances, reserving the right to ignore any that might possibly embarrass you.

13. Repeat the above experiments using modeling clay, interpreting the concepts of symmetry and asymmetry in all dimensions of your three-dimensional form. Study, observe, and compare as before. Do you prefer straight lines to curves? Do you prefer symmetrical or asymmetrical forms?

14. Consider your most interesting clay forms as an artistic abstraction. What connotations do you find in it? What connotations do other students find in it?

15. Using a sharp stick, a pencil, or a crayon, ornament your clay form in some way by imposing a design on its external surfaces. Does your design suggest other forms or experiences, e.g., the rhythmic alternation of two opposing forces, such as up and down or light and dark; the crossing of two paths; the flight of a bird; the spiral of a conch shell; the spiral of an experience that moves from its own center toward the periphery in ever-widening circles? Explain and discuss.

16. From your doodle designs, select two different forms that are interesting to you. Trace the outlines of these designs on colored construction paper, making several forms of various sizes. Cut out these paper forms and experiment with arranging them on a blank sheet of paper, pushing them around until you find a composition that is interesting to you. Does the composition suggest the rhythmic alternation of two opposing forces, like up and down. Or a spiral? Or some interaction between the two kinds of forms? Explain and discuss.

17. Pick up your paper forms and scatter them at random, keeping your eyes closed so that you will not be tempted to impose some order upon them. Study this random arrangement, asking the same questions as before. Then rearrange the forms into a composition that is interesting to you.

18. Select an artistically satisfying picture of a landscape or scene. Trace the outlines of the most evident forms in the pictures, eliminating all details. Study these outlines without referring to the picture. Which shapes are repeated? How are they varied in each repetition? How are the repeated shapes related to each other within the composition? What ideas are suggested by those relationships? Explain and discuss.

19. Using the basic outlines of these repeated forms, experiment with exaggerating and emphasizing them by elongating, diminishing, expanding, compressing, distorting, and coloring them in various ways. How are the ideas suggested by the relationships within the composition intensified, diminished, or modified by your experimental efforts?

20. Select stop-action pictures of a sport or dance performance and study them in the same way.

21. In terms of your own experience, ask yourself what the performer was probably thinking about at this point in the performance. Examine this conception in the same way you thought about your conception of a house, and try to sketch the basic outlines of your conception in the fewest possible pencil strokes.

22. In terms of your own experience, ask yourself what the performer was probably feeling at this point in the performance. Try to describe those feelings by explaining what they are like, e.g., a feeling of smooth-flowing rhythm, a sense of power, an explosive feeling of emotion, or the sense of feeling like a fish. Try to sketch the outlines of these conceptions in the fewest-possible lines, as you did with your conception of a home.

23. Consider these three sets of sketches simultaneously and ask how you might introduce your conceptions of thought and feeling into your outlines of the stop-action pictures. Experiment with this process until you produce a composition that is meaningful to you at all three levels of interpretation.

**24. Select the sport form or dance form that is most interesting to you. Over a period of time, think about your experiences with that form in terms of all three modes of interpretation. Record your thinking in words or sketches or in any way you choose. Some students have done this by recording sounds on tape, or they have thought about sounds that might be recorded and made notes about these for further study.

*25. In class, perform a series of national dances. (In my own classes I often use the Israeli dance *Mayim*, some version of the many Mediterranean dances performed to the music of *Miserlou*, and an American square dance such as *Texas Star*.) Try to analyze each of these dances in terms of the three modes of interpretation. How can you describe the patterns of the dance? What conceptions are denoted by the actions of the dancers? What conceptions may be connoted by certain SFRs you have recognized within the patterns of the dance?

*26. Either perform or recall a series of familiar sport forms, including one example from each of the classifications individual, dual, and team. Try to analyze each of these sports in terms of the three modes of interpretation, as above.

*27. In class, perform a series of exercises, including one that is used to develop strength, another that serves to develop endurance, and others that serve to stretch tissues or to promote relaxation. Try to analyze each of these exercises in terms of the three modes of interpretation, as above.

*28. Devise a new folk dance which might be appropriate to the interests of people of a given cultural background during some holiday season. Denote the basic patterns of your dance in some way, and try to explain the connotations you find in these patterns. It may be interesting to experiment with a culture other than your own or a holiday you do not normally celebrate in your own cultural pattern. If your classmates insist, teach them the dance and let them perform it.

*29. Choreograph a simple presentational dance, perhaps using the action patterns of a handshake or a greeting as the basis of your dance design. Denote and explain your patterns, as above. If you are reluctant to perform your own dance, do what Kor did; explain it to Dan and let him explain to you how he develops and performs the necessary coordinations within the movement patterns.

*30. Create a new sport-type game for children of a given age and a specified cultural milieu. Denote and explain your conceptions, as above. If possible, test your game by teaching it to an appropriate group of children, and ask them to tell you about their reactions to it.

*31. Create a new sport form for boys or girls of junior high school age. Denote and explain your conceptions, as above; if possible, submit your sport form to the test of performance.

*32. Consider the possibility that the people who will live on the "space platforms" of the future will need new kinds of exercises, games, sports, and dances. Try your hand at devising new forms appropriate to this environment, in which the pull of gravity is greatly diminished or negated.

*34. Explore the interactions within the learning process by devising and learning a new skill. (In class, I sometimes use the skill of tossing a crumpled wad of paper at a target placed in back of the thrower, perhaps limiting the coordination to an underarm or overarm throw.) After a series of trials, think about how you analyzed the task, how you devised the coordinations you used in your first attempt, and how you modified them in successive attempts.

*35. Explore the several stages within the learning process by teaching yourself a new skill that involves precise use of some small segment of the body. (For this purpose, my students have devised an individual game called toe ball. Using a small styrofoam or sponge-rubber ball, they attempt to propel it into a goal area by kicking it with the big toe of the preferred foot.)

After each trial, ask: Where was my attention focused during this attempt? What was I thinking about? How did I react to success or failure? Continue your trials until you have mastered the skill.

*36.   Explore the stages of the learning process further by trying to teach another adult the rudiments of toe ball. Ask him to analyze his efforts in the same way you did.

*37.   Explore the learning process further by trying to teach a trick, such as a tip-up or a somersault, to a dog and to a preschool-age child. Observe the reactions of both subjects within the learning process.

**38.   If you are now teaching, select some of the sketches or other forms you have developed in your continuing study of a sport form or dance form, as described under project 24, and present them to your own students in some way. Explain them as patterns and designs that you find in the sport or dance and ask what ideas they suggest. Then give your students an opportunity to develop their own patterns and designs, perhaps in class, as an outside assignment, or in their art classes. Display these presentational forms and let the students discuss them in their own way.

**39.   Review all the sketches and other forms you have developed in your own continuing study of one sport form or one dance form and bring your best ideas together in some representation of "this is how it seems to me." Bring these representations to class and discuss them.

During the past five years we have used some version of projects 38 and 39 at every instructional level from preschool through advanced graduate study. Without exception, the learners have found this experience meaningful, and many of our college students have commented, "Now, for the first time, I begin to understand what physical education is all about!" Therefore let me comment a bit further on this particular experience.

Initially, some students may resist this assignment on the grounds that it penalizes those who have no artistic ability or training. This resistance can be lessened by showing them simple and crude forms as well as those that do have artistic merit. It can also be lessened by making it clear that this assignment is not to be graded as an art form and by making it equally clear that there are no right or wrong answers in the ideas the students may present. It may also help if the teacher suggests a variety of media, including verbal and musical forms as well as graphic and plastic ones.

In general, however, we have encountered very little resistance to this assignment. As soon as the students are introduced to it by showing them a few samples, most of them become involved in this idea to a remarkable degree. And almost without exception they have been eager to display their own creations to the class and interested in the forms created by others.

Recently I had an opportunity to show pictures of some of these student-made forms to physical educators and their students in several non-English-speaking countries. In these situations, my own comments were necessarily limited, but everywhere the pictures spoke for themselves. Fencers got excited about "the meaning of fencing," swimmers responded immediately to representations of "what swimming means to me," and so on through the entire list of forms. Some students asked me to show the whole series again, and others called for repetitions of their favorites. Some instructors tried to persuade me to leave my packet of slide transparencies with them; others asked where they could buy a similar set for use in their own classes.

I think there might be some merit in developing a semipermanent collection of these nonverbal representations of meaning in sport and dance, and I hope you will suggest this possibility to any painters, sculptors, composers, and poets who might be interested in these important themes. Or perhaps you may know some moviemakers who would be interested in developing some of these ideas. (In part, this was done in the Japanese film of the 1964 Olympic games, but only in rather obvious terms.) Within the context of education, however, I think there is more merit in giving each student an opportunity to explore his own meanings in this way, and so I do not maintain a permanent collection of the forms my students have created. However, if you can persuade your students to part with them, you may want to keep a few particularly good examples, and perhaps you might display them from time to time to other educators who will find them of great interest.

Turning now to the question of collateral reading, this may range from the little brochure called *This Is Physical Education* (NEA-AAHPER, 1965) to an endless list of possible sources. In my undergraduate courses, I may confine my reading list to texts the students are using or have used in their classes in anatomy, physiology, psychology, education, or physical education; or, if time permits, I may direct the students to some of the references on the list I use in my graduate seminars.

In general, these references are selected with a view to developing a better understanding of the complexities of the SFRs involved in living, perceiving, feeling, thinking, moving, learning, and finding meaning. In each of these areas, the relevant literature is enormous, and new books and articles representing new advances in human understanding are appearing month by month. Thus I have never found it possible to develop a definitive list of references, and I shall not try to provide such a list here.

Rather, I usually offer my graduate students a representative list of names and titles in each area and then urge them to seek out their own references in the areas of inquiry which are of greatest interest to them. I may ask them to at least sample the literature in each of the several areas, but beyond that I usually let them concentrate their reading in whatever way they choose. Thus, the latter-day descendants of Sci read in science, Ven's adherents read in education, Pat's followers read in the arts, and those who find the thinking of Fil most interesting spend their time in the philosophy library.

In the general area of neurophysiological relationships, I usually list the names of such scientists as Wilder Penfield, Donald Hebb, Russell Brain, C. H. Waddington, H. G. Walter, J. Brownowski, Loren Eisley, Ernest Gellhorn, and Ragnar Granit; but there are many other scientists now writing about the processes of human thought and action. For reasons of historical interest, I usually include the writings of Kenneth Lashley, and I think every physical educator must sooner or later read *Man on His Nature*, the classic work of Sir Charles Sherrington, which is now available in many editions.

Within the general area of perception and cognition, any one of dozens of recent books may serve as a guide to further exploration. In this connection, I usually list the names of Gardner Murphy, Charles M. Solley, Howard S. Bartley, Karl U. Smith, William M. Smith, Bernard Berelson, and Gary Steiner. I have found *Elements of Psychology* (Knopf, 1962) by David Kretch and Richard Crutchfield useful as an elementary text, but there are also many others that are equally good. For reasons of historical interest, I always include some reference to the pioneering work of Jean Piaget, and I find *The Child's Conception of Space* (Routledge & Kegan Paul, 1963) by Jean Piaget and Barbel Inhelder useful for this purpose.

Among the many books and articles dealing with the processes involved in creating new ideas and translating them into new forms, Harold Rugg's *Imagination* (Harper & Row, 1963) is probably the best basic reference, but students may find it more meaningful if they encounter it later, rather than earlier, in their reading. The first part of Arthur Koestler's *The Act of Creation* (Macmillan, 1964) is also useful in this connection; and in the specific terms of art I like Herbert Read's *The Forms of Things Unknown* (Meridian, 1963).

The current list of books dealing with the concept of nonverbal communication and the connotational properties of nonverbal forms is endless. In general terms, some students may find the writings of Marshall McLuhan of interest; others may like Edward T. Hall's *The Silent Language* (Doubleday, 1959). In the specific terms of art, Susanne K. Langer's *Problems of Art* (Scribners, 1957) is a good nontechnical reference; and many students will find her *Feeling and Form* (Scribners, 1953) of particular interest. Here, too, I often list Herbert Read's *Icon and Idea* (Harvard University Press, 1955), Alexander Eliot's *Sight and Insight* (McDowell, Oblensky, 1959), Ben Shahn's *The Shape of Content* (Vintage, 1957) and R. G. Collingwood's *Principles of Art* (Galaxy, 1958).

In practice, I also use many elementary books that deal with the connotational properties of nonverbal and verbal forms in very simple terms. Some of these are "children's books," and others may not be readily available in your library, so let me list a few representative titles and publishers.

Fred Getting, *The Meaning and Wonder of Art* (Golden Press, 1963).

Harry Sternberg, *Composition: The Anatomy of Picture Making* (Pitman, 1958).

Langston Hughes, *The First Book of Rhythms* (Franklin Watts, 1954).

Langston Hughes, *The First Book of Jazz* (Franklin Watts, 1955).

Joost Merloo, *The Dance: From Ritual to Rock and Roll* (Chilton, 1960).

Arnold Haskell, *The Wonderful World of Dance* (Garden City, 1960).

Lois Ellfeldt, *A Primer for Choreographers* (National Press, 1967).

Helen Borten, *Do You Move As I Do?* (Abelard-Schuman, 1963).

John Ciardi, *How Does a Poem Mean?* (Houghton-Mifflin, 1959).

Tom Ziegler and H. Barnell, *The Zen of Base and Ball* (Simon and Schuster, 1964).

Juster Norton, *The Dot and the Line* (Random House, 1963).

Mary O'Neill and L. Weisgard, *Adventures in Color: Hailstones and Halibut Bones* (Doubleday, 1961).

In the general and technical literature of philosophy, I think it is important for the students to trace the emergence of our basic concern for the concepts of form, symbol, and meaning in Ernst Cassirer's *An Essay on Man* and Susanne K. Langer's *Philosophy in a New Key*, both of which are available in several editions. I also suggest that they read Lancelot Law Whyte's *Aspects of Form*, which has recently been reprinted by Midland Books. However, most students will find these monumental works more meaningful if they have already worked their way through the first three chapters of *Movement and Meaning*, so I usually defer these assignments until the middle of the course.

Beyond this, I do not try to structure their reading in philosophy. *Movement and Meaning* is developed within the context of certain existential and phenomenological schools of thought, but I think it would be unfortunate to confine the students' reading to the works of like-minded philosophers. Rather, I try to suggest the works of writers who will be congenial to the students' own philosophical or religious commitment, and I urge each student to pursue his search for meaning in his own chosen way.

In the general realm of education, virtually any recent book in the areas of curriculum and educational philosophy may serve as a meaningful reference, because virtually all educational writers are now dealing with the concepts of form, symbol, and meaning in some way. In this connection, the works of Jerome Bruner and Philip Phenix may be of particular interest. On occasion I have used various collections of readings on the learning process, including those edited by Lester and Alice Crow; by Theodore Harris and Wilson Schwan; and by Jerome Bruner, Jacqueline Goodnow, and George Austin. The series on the *Taxonomy of Educational Objectives*, edited by Benjamin S. Bloom, is also useful as a source of ideas, and most of the major publications issued under the imprint of the National Education Association are relevant to the interests of the students.

In the specific area of physical education, virtually any book, article, or research report may be relevant to some aspect of a student's interest in the relationships between movement and meaning. I have already mentioned the brochure *This Is Physical Education*, which I use as a standard reference in all courses; here let me add a few other recent works in which the movement-meaning relationships are approached directly. *Theory in Physical Education* (Lea and Febiger, 1963) by Camille Brown and Rosalind Cassidy is the first systematic attempt to analyze the conceptual framework of physical education as a field of scholarly study and research. In *The Phenomenology of Dance* (University of Wisconsin Press, 1966), Maxine Sheets has examined the SFRs of dance as an educational experience, and the experiential content of sport competition has been analyzed by Howard Slusher in *Man, Sport and Existence* (Lea and Febiger, 1967). Of course I also list my own *Connotations of Movement in Sport and Dance* (William C. Brown, 1965) and some of the papers that appeared before and after its publication. Of these, perhaps the most useful is the Amy Morris Homans Lecture, which appeared in the spring issue of *Quest*, 1967, under the title "How Does a Movement Mean?"

Regarding term papers and other written assignments, my own preference is for a series of essay-type papers which I call "Ideas and Insights." These may be about any idea the student has found interesting in his collateral reading or the class discussions. Usually, the students are somewhat dismayed by this unstructured assignment, and many of them make hard work of their first papers; but by the end of the course they enjoy this opportunity to explore their own thinking, and many of them discover talents for writing that they did not know they had. On the whole, their papers make interesting reading, and I have learned much from them, not only about the students but also about the topics under discussion.

In addition to these written assignments, I also schedule at least two 20-minute individual conferences with each student. In these conferences the student may talk about anything that interests him, but if he has difficulty getting started, I usually make some comment about his "Ideas and Insights" papers to start the conversation. In the second conference this is seldom necessary, because by then the students usually know what they want to talk about, and all I have to do is listen and toss in an occasional question or comment.

If the class is large, these individual conferences can be very time-consuming, but I have found them indispensable. Every student wants and needs an opportunity to talk about his own personal interests in dance, sports, and exercise; and it is difficult to find time for this in the class sessions. Then, too, I have learned much from these conferences, because the students have in-depth knowledge of many forms which I know only as a spectator, and my own personal experiences do not include high-level performance in dance or championship-level performance in sport. I ask the students to tell me about these experiences, and most of them welcome this opportunity to verbalize the content of their own thinking about these intensely meaningful aspects of their existence.

It has sometimes been said that physical educators are basically "nonverbal" people or that they tend to be more adept at nonverbal forms of expression. To some extent this may be true, as it is true about many people who work in the nonverbal arts, and I would add the generalization that they tend to be more interested in spatial relationships than most educators are. But given a vocabulary that is relevant to their own interests in movement, and an opportunity to use it, many students have become far more "verbal" about those interests and the meanings they find in them. As a consequence of this development of their verbal skills, many of them have reported that they find it easier to communicate with their own students and colleagues about the kinds of concepts and meanings that are developed within the curriculum of physical education.

Since this was my major purpose in writing *Movement and Meaning*, you will understand why I hope you will also adapt some of these teaching techniques to your own educational goals and purposes.

For your convenience, I am also listing the titles of the

poems from which the quotations at the beginning of each section of the book were taken. All references are to *The Collected Poems of Wallace Stevens* (Alfred A. Knopf, Inc., 1954), but the individual poems may be found in many other sources.

Title page: "Connoisseur of Chaos," p. 215.

Preface: "An Ordinary Evening in New Haven," p. 488.

Forms: "A Primitive like an Orb," p. 443.

Man-made Forms: "Things of August," pp. 494–495.

Man-made Movement Forms: "A Primitive like an Orb," p. 442; "Sad Strains of a Gay Waltz," p. 122.

Sources of Meaning in Movement: "Looking across the Fields and Watching the Birds Fly," p. 518.

Dance Forms: "Bouquet of Roses in Sunlight," p. 430.

Sport Forms: "Six Significant Landscapes," p. 74.

Exercise Forms: "Of Modern Poetry," p. 239.

"Learning to Move—Moving to Learn": "Looking across the Fields and Watching the Birds Fly," p. 518.

Appendix for Educators: "Notes toward a Supreme Fiction," p. 395.

INDEX

INDEX